Debating in Teaching and Learning English

Also available from Bloomsbury

Teaching Listening and Speaking in Second and Foreign Language Contexts,
Kathleen M. Bailey

Debating in Teaching and Learning English

Theory and Practice for Pedagogy and Curriculum

Ben Wilson

BLOOMSBURY ACADEMIC
LONDON • NEW YORK • OXFORD • NEW DELHI • SYDNEY

BLOOMSBURY ACADEMIC
Bloomsbury Publishing Plc, 50 Bedford Square, London, WC1B 3DP, UK
Bloomsbury Publishing Inc, 1359 Broadway, New York, NY 10018, USA
Bloomsbury Publishing Ireland, 29 Earlsfort Terrace, Dublin 2, D02 AY28, Ireland

BLOOMSBURY, BLOOMSBURY ACADEMIC and the Diana logo
are trademarks of Bloomsbury Publishing Plc

First published in Great Britain 2024
Paperback edition published 2026

Copyright © Ben Wilson, 2024, 2026

Ben Wilson has asserted his right under the Copyright, Designs and
Patents Act, 1988, to be identified as Author of this work.

For legal purposes the Acknowledgements on p. x constitute
an extension of this copyright page.

Cover design: Grace Ridge
Cover image: Federica Marzolo

All rights reserved. No part of this publication may be: i) reproduced or transmitted in any form, electronic or mechanical, including photocopying, recording or by means of any information storage or retrieval system without prior permission in writing from the publishers; or ii) used or reproduced in any way for the training, development or operation of artificial intelligence (AI) technologies, including generative AI technologies. The rights holders expressly reserve this publication from the text and data mining exception as per Article 4(3) of the Digital Single Market Directive (EU) 2019/790.

Bloomsbury Publishing Plc does not have any control over, or responsibility for, any third-party websites referred to or in this book. All internet addresses given in this book were correct at the time of going to press. The author and publisher regret any inconvenience caused if addresses have changed or sites have ceased to exist, but can accept no responsibility for any such changes.

A catalogue record for this book is available from the British Library.

Library of Congress Cataloging-in-Publication Data

Names: Wilson, Ben (Independent researcher), author.
Title: Debating in teaching and learning English : theory and practice for
pedagogy and curriculum / Ben Wilson.
Description: London ; New York : Bloomsbury Academic, 2024. | Includes bibliographical references and index. | Summary: "Debating is a well-known method of dialogic speaking and is widely practiced, intercontinentally and across diverse cultural boundaries, to develop interaction, negotiation, agreeing and disagreeing in TEFL. This book invites scholars and practitioners to reflect on the demands of the current age for moving forward educational practice. It examines how debating can promote a holistic understanding and improvement of experience of education, and indeed academic outcomes. The author details the experiences of an adult EFL debate group in a private language school in the North of Italy, reporting how the participants experience the pedagogy, so as to offer insights into it as a form of teaching speaking in adult EFL"– Provided by publisher.
Identifiers: LCCN 2023046675 (print) | LCCN 2023046676 (ebook) | ISBN 9781350413566 (hardback) | ISBN 9781350413573 (paperback) | ISBN 9781350413597 (epub) | ISBN 9781350413580 (ebook)
Subjects: LCSH: English language–Study and teaching–Foreign speakers. | Debates and debating–Study and teaching. | Adult education.
Classification: LCC PE1128.A2 W538 2024 (print) | LCC PE1128.A2 (ebook) |
DDC 420.71/5–dc23/eng/20240108
LC record available at https://lccn.loc.gov/2023046675
LC ebook record available at https://lccn.loc.gov/2023046676

ISBN: HB: 978-1-3504-1356-6
PB: 978-1-3504-1357-3
ePDF: 978-1-3504-1358-0
eBook: 978-1-3504-1359-7

Typeset by Integra Software Services Pvt. Ltd.

For product safety related questions contact productsafety@bloomsbury.com.

To find out more about our authors and books visit www.bloomsbury.com
and sign up for our newsletters.

The day is approaching when all the peoples of the world will have adopted one universal language and one common script. When this is achieved, to whatsoever city a person may journey, it shall be as if they were entering their own home. These things are obligatory and absolutely essential. It is incumbent upon every person of insight and understanding to strive to translate that which hath been written into reality and action.

(Bahá'u'lláh)

If five people meet together to seek for truth, they must begin by cutting themselves free from all their own special conditions and renouncing all preconceived ideas. In order to seek for truth we must give up our prejudices, our own small trivial notions; an open receptive mind is essential. If our chalice is full of self, there is no room in it for the water of life. The fact that we imagine ourselves to be right and everybody else wrong is the greatest of obstacles in the path towards unity, and unity is necessary if we would reach truth, for truth is one.

(Abdul Bahà)

Contents

List of Figures	viii
List of Tables	ix
Acknowledgements	x
Introduction	1
1 EFL Learning and the Role of Speaking	7
2 A History of Teaching the Spoken Language in EFL	13
3 A Brief History of Debating	25
4 Dialogic Teaching and Second Language Acquisition	35
5 Debating, Dialogic Teaching and Affect in Teaching and Learning English	49
6 Debate Curriculum and Pedagogy	65
7 The Debate Curriculum and Pedagogy: What We Did	69
8 Debating as a Process	87
9 An Integrated Curriculum and Pedagogy for Debating	131
Conclusion	145
Glossary	154
Bibliography	155
Index	168

Figures

1 Four pointed star of educational experience 70
2 The process of debating 88

Tables

1	Teacher assessment overview	41
2	Pre- and post-interview debate structure	67
3	The continuity of the lesson debate course cycle	133

Acknowledgements

I would like to thank my supervisors and friends at Teesside University and the staff at Bloomsbury Academic for their kind support and encouragement. In particular to Maria Giovanna Brauzzi, Susan Furber, Laura Gallon, Clive Hedges, Sarah McDonald, Saaed Muhammed and especially Sally Neaum.

Thank you to all those involved in the debating group and staff where the debates were held and those others who gave invaluable support: Ibrahim Ali Omer Bayoud, Maureen Chester, Dave Dignam, Sean Grimes, Gianni Grimaldi, Fiorenzo Labocetta, Federica Marzolo, Washington Oquendo, Ian & Catherine Wilson, F. T. Wilson-Marzolo, Marina Zacco and all of the friends of the ASL of Genoa.

Introduction

Speaking is the most automatic form of communication for most people. We often take for granted our ability to speak, and most of us are unaware of the great complexity that lies behind our learning of grammar, vocabulary, phonetics etc. It is perhaps for these reasons that our ability in speaking emerges without us noticing our progress or achievements. And yet, our different roles in society may place a staggeringly diverse set of demands on this capacity to express ourselves, of what we know, and indeed to engage with others' expression of themselves and what they know. It is perhaps not until we learn a second language that we begin to become aware of the structure and peculiarities of our language(s), how we feel about using them, and our motivations for using them. Moreover, we are perhaps also unaware of just how challenging it can be to express thought in a new language: this is the main objective and main challenge for most second language learners (Thiriau, 2017). Speaking is perhaps one of the most-prized abilities that we possess – and yet – to a greater or lesser extent it is surely something that is rarely fully appreciated.

The greatest surprise then, may come in discovering that despite its importance – it is among English language learners and teachers – still the most difficult aspect of language learning by far and therefore represents a real challenge as the value of learning spoken English increases for a variety of important needs (Kubanyiova, 2018). One major insight from recent research into speaking is that the psychology of the learner and teacher plays a key role in creating suitable conditions under which English language learners can succeed in this aim (Dornyei & Ryan, 2015; Mercer, 2018; Dewaele et al., 2019). More specifically, the language learner should feel that they are in a safe speaking environment that they feel comfortable in (Kubanyiova, 2018). The creation of such a social context is partly dependent on the psychology of the group dynamics which rely on the social psychological personal-social relations of the language classroom (Dornyei & Ryan, 2015). As such, researching the ways in which teachers can work with curriculum and pedagogy to create such positive learning environments to enhance both acquisition and experience is desirable (Kubanyiova, 2018).

This book is about adult speaking practices and methods, which include the role of topics and curriculum. It is about using debate to develop foreign language or other language speaking, and its central role within language pedagogy. As an English language teacher, it has been written for other language teachers, including those with an academic interest in language, method and curriculum. It is also for teachers and teacher-researchers who are interested in speaking as a form of literacy, as speaking forms a part of the broader literacy practices of learners in society, including young adults and potentially teenagers. It might be mainly of interest to practitioners working in contexts where English is a second or foreign language, as was the case in the contexts in which I have mainly worked and researched, although it may also be equally of interest to ESOL (English to speakers of other languages) contexts where English is the main language.

Based on my varied experiences across a range of both teaching English as a foreign language (TEFL) and teaching English to speakers of other languages (TESOL) contexts, I had become interested in what seemed to be the potential of dialogic speaking as key in unlocking and initiating teacher-student and student-student communication in the classroom. I perceived this as a way of beginning an educational process that could maximize all of the other dimensions of the English language teaching-learning experience. One aspect of this which seemed fundamental was creating positive affective conditions in which students were happy with the experience of their education. I began to read about the role of affect, sometimes referred to as humanism, but more recently as positive psychology, and believed that based on my experience at that point in my teaching career, small group discussions seemed to possess the most potential to afford these benefits. My guiding philosophy of education as a teacher was, therefore, the importance of this dimension in education – which ultimately belongs to the larger issues associated with the role of psychology in Second Language Acquisition (SLA) (Dewaele et al., 2019). Attention is drawn here, however, to the role of psychology and SLA with respect to language instruction, itself a part of SLA studies, and one of the main areas of research alongside the nature of learner language, the learner's developing language (interlanguage), social aspects of interlanguage, discourse aspects of interlanguage, linguistic aspects of interlanguage and individual differences in L2 acquisition (Ellis, 2013).

The main argument, however, that I would like to make, is that Debating could be employed as an effective, and indeed, a positive affective form of dialogic speaking in EFL and ESOL provisions. I have done this by researching a group of EFL students in which debating was the main form of pedagogy, and situated this context among secondary research into the teaching of speaking through debate as dialogic speaking. The second argument is that it is rather a consideration of the humanistic-affective dimension within a holistic model of instruction that considers the whole educational experience that should form the basis of a philosophy of education, given what is now known about education and the role of psychology. The sum of which entails that each major dimension of the overall educational experience is taken into account in planning pedagogy and curriculum (Curran, 1972; Farid Arbab, 2016). This is to say that teachers should be informed about the psychology of the learner, and indeed about their own psychology as teachers (Curran, 1969, 1972; Friere, 1972; Mercer, 2018).

The term 'EFL' is used to indicate when the English language is being learned in a country where English is not the first language, and the term 'TEFL' refers to Teaching EFL. This form of learning and teaching applies to the majority of contexts referred to in this book. The term 'English as a second language' (ESL) is sometimes used to refer to this same group of learners, however, it does not account for the many learners who already speak a number of other languages, therefore the more general term – EFL – is more widely used. The term 'ESOL' refers to learners who are learning in a country where English is often the first language and where they may speak more than one language, thus often rendering the application of the term 'ESL' inaccurate. As such the categories ESOL and EFL are taken to be the most widely used, apart from in North America where ESL has been preferred in adult English language learning contexts. In recent years both the terms 'EAL' (English as an additional language), and 'ENL' (English as a new language) have been employed – though more often in state schools. The participants in this book were adult EFL learners, and therefore I was involved in TEFL. In Italy, these are those who have voluntarily chosen to partake in some form of formal education within a private language school or university that caters to this age group. Adults are defined as those who are eighteen years old or above, the members of the debate group being retired individuals.

Chapter 1 introduces the main two pillars of the book that rest on debating as dialogic speaking, and the role of affect – in relation to utilizing debating as a form of pedagogy – and particularly in EFL teaching with adults. Chapter 2 explores the history of teaching the spoken language in EFL up until the present day. Chapter 3 describes a history of debating by following the dominant religious-academic traditions that can be seen to have influenced philosophy, which in turn influenced the eventual employment of it in education. Chapter 4 examines the relationship between dialogic teaching and affect. The relationship between affect and dialogic teaching is surveyed via a historical perspective that leads to the current state of contemporary research into affect and speaking in adult EFL. Chapter 5 examines the relationship between debating as a form of dialogic speech and its interplay with the affective dimension in teaching and learning English. In Chapter 6, the evolution of the debate curriculum and pedagogy – the context in which the research took place – is introduced. The debate participant and the initial pedagogy and curriculum are described. In Chapter 7, the findings from the interviews as conceived and categorized into the communicative, educational, cognitive and social experiences of debating are presented. The experiences consist mainly of the affective experience of debating as a form of teaching-learning speaking in EFL. Chapter 8 harmonizes the findings alongside the insights from previous chapters in order to show how debating can be considered as a form of dialogic speaking that can afford positive affective experience which appeals to the four dimensions of education laid out in the previous chapter. Key aspects of the four experiences are shown to contain a variety of penetrating insights into the affective consequences of the pedagogy and curriculum. Chapter 9 provides a mini-curriculum and a basic lesson plan overview for teachers to either adapt or adopt as a complete curriculum. In addition, a textbook-style set of four lessons is given as a more specific example of how each lesson could be designed. The final chapter seeks to bring together the various insights derived from both the secondary and primary research and discuss the implications for the teaching of speaking in EFL and the use of debating in EFL more broadly.

The personal challenge involved with language learning is largely social in character – when the concern is to develop speaking (Kubanyiova, 2018). However, participating as an actor in the social world necessarily involves the personal, individual, subjective sense of self – and therefore the psychology of the learner is inseparable from the social world in which they inhabit. This is the claim of Curran (1972) who argued that the concept in psychology regarding the divided self was very much applicable to the psychology of language learning and teaching (1969, 1972). The approach taken in this book is to seek how the psychology of the learner – and indeed the teacher – can be made whole – within the individual and consequently within the group. This objective involves a process through which the learner and the teacher become a friend to themselves, by continually reflecting, counselling and understanding

(Curran, 1969). Debating, in the manner proposed in this book, may be one such effective and positively affective means by which the vital skill of speaking could be cultivated in the language classroom. It requires a personal sense of self-acceptance of what being a learner entails, alongside the acceptance of one's role in a community of learners when they share the same goal of improving their language skills. It is also, therefore, incumbent on teachers to understand the experience of the learner to facilitate this process and recognize the other aspects of their role (Curran, 1972; Freire, 1974; Mercer, 2018).

The approach in this book to discovering more about these issues is by *asking speakers about their experiences* of debating, which could take into account their perspectives of the whole experience as a language learner, and sharpen and clarify the findings from the purely cognitive, non-social, or emotional perspective. That such a holistic approach could be warranted due to the lack of a single educational theory in existence heretofore (Farid-Arbab, 2016). This book will provide an example of how in my case, a practitioner can research their teaching practice so as to shed light on some ways in which the building of such consideration – while always being contingent on contextual issues that only teachers can have the complete expert experience and knowledge to perceive – can support practice, and perhaps provide ways in which other practitioners may experiment, as a way of improving outcomes for themselves and their students (Burns, 2010).

1

EFL Learning and the Role of Speaking

In the Western world, speaking in public as a form of dialogue and often debate was practised and argued to promote a healthy society by Socrates, Plato and Aristotle, and was also argued to be an art form of great moral importance that would be a characteristic of the democratic nature of society (Golden, 2003). However, the importance of it has formed a part of ancient cultures going back much further in history, with Socrates himself being said to have been influenced by the Jewish religious culture of the time (Bahà'u'llah, 1993; Abdul Bahà, 2011). Further east, it has found distinct expression through Buddhist traditions (Perdue, 2014), and indeed as the result of each progressive religion, evolved in character over many thousands of years (Fakrhy, 1983; Esslemont, 2006; Perdue, 2014). Since at least the nineteenth century, its roots in religion have been marginalized in the West, though an awareness in such as Catholicism where its heritage and current practice persist, and can be seen in Jesuit philosophy and Thomism (McBrien, 1994; Kerr, 2002).

Teaching and learning the spoken language, in recent centuries, grew out of an increased amount of international travel and trade, and occurred alongside the Industrial Revolution (Howatt & Smith, 2014). Though initially, speaking was based on traditional methods of studying grammar and translating texts, it eventually arrived at a turning point in the 1970s, in language teaching studies that began to argue it was a moral imperative for rebalancing power relations between teacher and student, towards a dialogic communicative dynamic, and away from a traditional transmissive form of education. This, interestingly, coincided with a revolution in attitude towards classroom dynamics in language teaching brought about by proponents of humanistic approaches and methods (Larsen Freeman & Anderson, 2011). More recently, dialogic speaking has been promoted as a fundamentally vital form of communication that affords cognitive and intellectual development in young people within state educational contexts globally (Alexander, 2006, 2020), with renewed efforts combining these insights about classroom communication with the significance of positive psychological relations (Arnold, 2011; Dornyei & Ryan, 2015; Farid-Arbab, 2016).

Speaking in English as a foreign language is most often associated with *oracy* which is defined by it being a dialogic form of speaking, and speech-based. This is in contrast with *rhetoric* which is monologic and can be verbal and non-verbal, expressed via a variety of mediums. Both, however, have played an important role in education and language education over the centuries, and the dividing line between the two is sometimes debated (Kern, 2010).

The aims of this kind of speaking were to develop the individual's capacity to argue, communicate effectively and teach, one of the earliest and most cited examples being found in Aristotle's *The Art of Rhetoric* (see Aristotle, 2012). Later on in history, during the Middle Ages, rhetoric became a part of *the trivium* which incorporated the study of logic and grammar within a liberal arts education. Its emphasis was on language and communication as basic but fundamental skills that were foundational for the study of other subjects (Gaunt & Stott, 2019). During modern and contemporary times, oracy has overtaken rhetoric, as democracy in education and the role of speaking have become more recognized through research. The extent to which this has found its way into practice is dependent on local contexts, however, with some nations employing this method more than others (Alexander, 2006). Technology has also greatly accelerated the practice of oracy, as engagement with media has increased through social media which involves dialogic speech, and goes beyond the more restricted capacities of radio and television (Levin & Moses Hines, 2003).

In English language teaching studies, oracy remains a key priority for developing the second or other languages, with mounting research highlighting the affordances of verbal communication for both academic and professional purposes (Evans & Jones, 2007), from a focus on developing a speech for functional communication and conversation, to more recently in adult EFL contexts through debating (Aclan & Aziz, 2015).

Dialogic speaking and debating

Since the increase in focus on communication began at the dawn of the Communicative language learning era in the 1970s conversation and more particularly, dialogic communication became valued as the main form of assessing speaking in language exams, and is popular with language learners, as a way of improving their language speaking skills (Whong, 2011; Hughes & Szczepek-Reed, 2017). The term 'dialogue' refers to the type of speaking that is argued for in this book, as an effective and potentially positive-affective way of teaching and learning a second language which can be afforded by debating as EFL pedagogy. This involves the way in which the teacher engages with students and the way in which students engage with each other and the teacher (Alexander, 2020). It also:

> harnesses the power of talk to engage students' interest, stimulate their thinking, advance their understanding, expand their ideas, and build and evaluate an argument, empowering them for lifelong learning and for social and democratic engagement.
>
> (Alexander, 2020, 1)

Debating as a form of dialogic speaking – in its broadest sense – refers to a discussion in which individuals share their points of view on a given topic, based on their experience and factual knowledge (Al-asmari & Salahuddin, 2012). It does not refer to a particular type of formalized debate – among the many varieties – but to an agreed format between the chair and the participants (Al-Mahrooqi & Tabakow, 2015). One major way in which debating can be divided into two approaches is the traditionally competitive variety versus the collaborative. A consideration when selecting a particular approach as a teacher is which of these two different approaches learners have a preference for and from a psychological and language educational perspective which increases student engagement; the main challenge facing teachers and learners in classroom speaking today (Kubanyiova, 2018).

Affect

'Humanism' and 'affect' are terms that have both been used in the past, to describe the same dimension of language education, with some scholars opting for the term 'humanistic', such as Freire (1972) and Stevick (1990), while others have used the term 'affect', including Curran (1972) and Arnold (2011). In more recent years, the term 'positive-psychology' has been employed, alongside emerging calls for its import in second language acquisition and teaching (Dewaele et al., 2019). While these terms have been challenging to define in psychology and education (Stevick, 1990), one broad definition offers a way of initially situating its role; it has been said to represent:

> (the) struggle for the primacy of the individual personality against deterministic behaviorist emphases ... students are encouraged to talk about themselves, to be open with others, and to express their feelings.
>
> (Rivers, 1983 in Stevick, 1990)

However, this book will explore how learner experiences of debating can be understood as correlating to more specific humanistic criteria as defined mainly by Curran (1972) and Freire (1972, 1974). I will draw on both terms, but in different ways: the term 'affective' will refer to the affective dimension of language education, wherein, I refer to both positive and negative affect. Humanism, on the other hand, and humanistic teaching denote a positive affective approach or method. In contrast, but sometimes conflated with concepts of humanism and affect, the term 'holistic' is used. Holism or whole-person itself is also considered as comprising the dimension of humanism or positive affect in a given model, approach or method of education.

Dialogic speaking, debating and affect

Beyond the historical perspective, research into teaching adults to speak a foreign language is characterized in different ways; from the diverging psychological approaches which are heavily focused on cognition to the external social dimensions (Hughes, 2002; Hughes & Szczepek-Reed, 2017). Little research has been carried out into the experiential-affective perspective, however, and that which has been investigated is mostly limited to exploring the extent and role of anxiety, for example Baran-Łucarz, 2014; Setiawan, 2018; Liu & Xiangming, 2019. As such, one of the motivations for new research is to gain an understanding of adult learner experience of speaking in EFL from a broader experiential perspective – not just limited to anxiety. After all, a human being's language use fulfils many important functions:

> from the material to the intellectual, for the mediation of personal relationships, the expression of feelings, and so on. Language in all these uses has come within one's own direct experience, and because of this one is subconsciously aware that language has many functions that affect one personally. Language is ... a rich and adaptable instrument for the realization of one's intentions; there is hardly any limit to what one can do with it.
>
> (Halliday, 1976, 10)

While there has been an increasing interest in debating as a form of pedagogy in first language state schools, and also in TEFL state school contexts, there is a much smaller body of research into adult TEFL debating (Akerman & Neale, 2011; Cinganotto, 2019). In addition, there is an even smaller amount that has researched debating as a form of teaching speaking in EFL from the experiential perspective. This situation reflects a broader concern that there is very little research into issues of second language acquisition from the holistic or affective perspective and that this lack of research limits the insights from the often opposing purely cognitive or socially orientated research (Dufva, 2013). In this same sense, a broader holistic-experiential approach seeks to widen the limited perspectives inherent in scientism in relation to human behaviour (Habermas, 1972; Horkheimer, 1972); an essential objective in today's world (OECD, 2021). Fundamentally, this involves considering EFL speaking from the perspective of the speaker and not only from the perspective of the practitioner or researcher.

This is one of the reasons why communication, and more specifically – dialogue – as an approach to a fundamental alternative to the kind of pedagogy associated with traditional education – is still considered today to be an important consideration, in guiding debates about education (Chomsky, 2002; Farid-Arbab, 2016). Indeed, it is considered to be fundamental in teaching and learning languages (Freire, 1974; Scrivener, 2005; Barton et al., 2010), especially in contrast to uncritically using textbook speaking exercises or lesson plans from the internet which may not be always so closely attuned to the interests of students (Nguyen & Hung, 2020). Indeed, with debating, it is necessary to learn about the participant's interests to create an ongoing curriculum. In a similar manner, it has also become evident over time that the pedagogy itself is most successful when teachers enquire at the beginning of a course what the communicative goals of the learners are. This is particularly important given the centrality of speaking as a skill in developing a foreign language (Swain, 1995; Swain & Lapkin, 1995; Thiriau, 2017), and the associated cognitive (Hughes, 2002) and affective challenges that require practice to develop (Curran, 1972; Thiriau, 2017).

Chapter summary

In recent years, there has been an increase in the focus on dialogic speaking in education, as an appropriate form of pedagogy given the knowledge provided by a variety of studies within second language acquisition and language teaching.

Its role at the societal level is taken to be of great import, though individual skills such as critical thinking, personal development and well-being in a democratic context are key. While such values have played a part in many societies since ancient times, a resurgence in their significance came into play with the emergence of the Communicative language era during the 1970s which was a seminal period for humanistic developments in language teaching. One motivation for this intervention was the increasing recognition of older traditional methods lacking in what were considered new insights into language pedagogy. Indeed, the momentum created – in part – by technological advances and their relationship with media usage appears to be driving an increase in human dialogue. As a consequence of this spirit and the advances of the age, debating has re-emerged, albeit slowly, as a form of dialogue worthy of employment in education, due to the aforementioned affordances associated with dialogic speech. Despite these encouraging moves, more research is needed that is fit to inform both local and wider educational practices, for the benefits of debating and dialogic speaking to become embedded in language education more pervasively. One way in which future research could provide a deeper understanding of the psychological affordances associated with affect which entail such factors as personal growth, and increased confidence which are highly desirable for the development of speaking is to learn from learners and teachers about their experiences and attitudes towards the proposed approaches to dialogic speaking and debating.

In order to clarify the contemporary perspectives on teaching and learning speaking in EFL, a history of the development of these practices will be presented, so as to situate the key issues raised regarding debating as dialogic speech as a potentially humanistic approach to teaching speaking. This will be the focus of the next chapter.

2

A History of Teaching the Spoken Language in EFL

Regarding its history in the Western world, it is suggested that the history of language teaching goes back to the 1700s in Europe, and has been divided into four main periods which express the main concerns and overall approaches among teaching theories and practices, as opposed to very specific methods: the classical period (1750–1880); the reform period (1880–1920); the scientific period (1920–70); and the communicative period (1970–2000+) (Howatt & Smith, 2014).

The classical period

The first period known as the classical period was mainly concerned with modern language teaching in Europe and was not specifically focused on the teaching of only English, but also other languages. Indeed, it was not until the beginning of the third era that a shift in this direction would occur. The main method associated with this approach is often termed either the 'grammar-translation method' or the 'classical method' and the main concern was emulating the teaching of classical languages. These two methods shared the objective of learning the language via translation so as to enable the reading of Greek and Latin literature. As Latin lost its place as the lingua franca of Europe however, the utility of teaching Latin was questioned, and along with it the methods used. The vernacular languages replaced Latin and therefore in order to communicate and read each other's literature, more Europeans began to learn each other's languages. At one point French was dominant, but as the population of Britain and the United States grew exponentially during this era, it led to greater attention being paid to learning English. Furthermore, as a consequence of the increased ease of travel throughout the European continent, a greater need was brought about for learning the spoken language. Given its focus on reading and writing, the grammar-translation method was found wanting in this respect and began to lose favour with those whose primary goals as foreign language learners were to travel and communicate verbally (Howatt & Smith, 2014).

The reform period

The reform period that took place between 1880 and 1920 signals the end of a focus on teaching in Europe and the beginning of teaching on an international level. An emphasis on teaching the spoken language was expressed via a number of methods, including the natural method, and later the Berlitz method. There were two types of reform during this period: one which affected the secondary school system in Europe and the other private language teaching in the United States. These reforms also focused on teaching the spoken language due to the fact that the method was targeted at and used by everyday people and not only the elites who had previously been the only class to have access to such education. The method was labelled the natural method, then the Berlitz method, after its originator, though it would eventually become more widely known as the direct method. Berlitz himself relocated to Europe where he founded what would eventually become the Berlitz chain of language schools which still exists today. What aided this drive towards an emphasis on the spoken language were developments in the science of phonetics, thus signalling an early example of applied linguistics in language teaching. Indeed, the Direct Method and science would continue to inform teaching in the next major era (Howatt & Smith, 2014).

The scientific period

The third, scientific period's (1920–70) core concern was the scientific basis for teaching. This followed on from the reform period's introduction of phonetics, as further consideration of linguistics was brought into play, as was, though to a lesser degree learning theories from psychology (Howatt & Smith, 2014). This informed:

> The basis for the selection of vocabulary and, later, grammatical 'structures' or 'patterns' which had received a lot of attention. By the end of the period, key features of all good teaching practice were considered to be the use of drills (rote

learning of repeated phrases) and exercises aimed explicitly at the formation of correct habits in the production of grammatical structures which had themselves been scientifically selected.

(Howatt & Smith, 2014, 85)

Linguistics in American universities was grounded in an empiricist philosophy in which description and the production of taxonomies of languages were central (Chomsky & Halle, 1965). Such research included ethnographic studies into the language of as were then unchartered cultures, such as in Papua New Guinea carried out by Malinowski and other structural anthropologists (O'Reilly, 2009). In this sense, language was studied as an external and therefore social and communicative phenomenon; the psychological school of Behaviourism being dominant at the time. This trend, though in different ways was reflected in the language teaching practices at the time, whereby students were expected to learn the known grammar and vocabulary of a target language according to the descriptions of them that had been amassed (Richards & Rodgers, 2014). The methods that expressed this new perspective were the oral method, the multiple line of approach, the situational approach, the oral approach and the audiolingual method (Howatt & Smith, 2014). During these years in which Behaviourism was dominant, two of these methods could be seen to reflect the two most clearly different dimensions of how language teaching was informed by the social sciences. Firstly, the audiolingual method was perhaps one of the major language teaching methods and is considered the archetypal method of this time. This method evidenced the concept of conditioning found in Behaviourism and expressed itself in the rote learning of grammar and vocabulary, and repetition by drilling exercises. The second method, the situational approach, perhaps more naturally reflected actual usage in that it taught oral communication through role play in mimicking real-life situations. Ultimately, however, both methods adopted Behaviourism's belief that rote learning of sentences was sufficient for learning a foreign language (Larsen-Freeman & Anderson, 2011). However, in the following era, a major shift would occur that challenged this.

The communicative period

The communicative period beginning in around 1970 and still present today is argued to have occurred mainly due to the paradigm shift in psychology and linguistics that began in the late 1950s. However, this period is also known for introducing the consideration of dialogic speaking, most notably as argued for by Freire (1972, 1974), and the humanistic dimension which was informed by developments in humanistic psychology (Larsen-Freeman & Anderson, 2011), also notably attributed to Freire (1972, 1974) and Curran (1972, 1976, 1978).

Regarding the cognitive dimension of what led to this period Noam Chomsky's critique of one of the major Behaviourist thinkers of the time, Skinner (1957) is often taken to represent the moment in which this break began (Larsen-Freeman & Anderson, 2011). With respect to linguistics, Chomsky's view was that one of the major and notable attributes of language was its creativity and not its predictability as Skinner had argued (Chomsky, 1959). As such, rote learning of stock sentences as a method of second or other language learning was challenged. Instead, exposure to the language in a natural manner through opportunities for natural conversation was believed to more accurately mimic the child's acquisition of the first language (the L1), and also the teenager or the adults of the L2. By the 1970s Chomsky's insights had gained momentum and contributed to the shift into the communicative period, even though Chomsky made no claim of how his work in formal linguistics could inform language teaching. Indeed, he denied that his work could inform language teaching; instead, professing that teachers could aid learning by helping to stimulate students and motivating them (Chomsky, 1988). While spoken communication retained its value in what would become the fourth and present paradigm, 'the communicative period', it differed in its linguistic and psychological rationale from the previous era's influence from Behaviourism, and this influenced the style of speaking and listening in language teaching methods, in which freer, more natural conversation communication was introduced into the classroom (Larsen-Freeman & Anderson, 2011).

One notable interpreter of Chomsky's work in linguistics however was the second language acquisition (SLA) theorist Krashen who formulated the natural method (Krashen & Terrel, 2000). Krashen's input hypothesis argued that SLA is mainly dependent on exposure to the discourse of the target language which is one stage ahead of the learner's current stage (Krashen, 1985). That exposure to input is necessary for SLA has therefore become one of the central tenets of SLA that are said should inform language teaching (Whong, 2011). Krashen termed this language as 'comprehensible input': the best way of attaining his proposal would be for a student to attend language classes in which the curriculum and pedagogy would feature some unknown structures or vocabulary, situated among familiar languages (Krashen, 1985). Krashen's emphasis on language input was however at odds with the main emphasis of the communicative period on output. Though there was a social dimension of language teaching in Krashen's proposals insofar as he proposed that learners attend language classes with other students, it was not based on the main tenets of social interactionism, or functional and cognitive linguistics which emphasize dialogue, or the agency or autonomy of the learner (Whong, 2011). In this sense, Krashen's model for language teaching could be deemed more of a teacher-centred content model as opposed to a student-centred process model, the latter being favoured by cognitive and functional approaches to teaching (Coffin, Donahue, & North, 2009; Rose & Martin, 2012;). Krashen's theory therefore set up a stark contrast between a relatively passive receptive-orientated model of acquisition, versus an active communicative-productive position. More recently, Krashen's theory is drawn on by Lantolf and Thorne's (2006) constructivist approach to the second language development model that is based on Vygotsky's cultural-historical psychology.

Attempts to apply insights from linguistics shaped what would become the emerging sub-discipline of applied linguistics (Howatt & Smith, 2014) and represented a shift in the 1970s which brought about the beginning of the communicative period (Larsen-Freeman & Anderson, 2011). The linguistic dimension when translated into teaching practice can therefore be termed the 'language' dimension and has been the main focus of most research and practice in language teaching research (Whong, 2011).

Another development that informed communicative language teaching (CLT) but had not been explicit in any previous era or method did not come from linguistics, however. Informed by humanistic developments in psychology during the 1960s due to Rogers (Stevick, 1990), humanistic or affective factors were argued to be fundamental in promoting effective language acquisition, as they promoted positive learning experience, which entailed engaging the personality and interests of the learner (Curran, 1972; Freire, 1972; Moscowitz, 1978; Stevick, 1980). Indeed, by the 1980s Krashen had also formulated his own conception of this, namely in the affective-filter metaphor. Affective factors such as motivation, personality, attitude and emotional factors – all psychological in nature – were argued to increase or reduce the acquisition of comprehensible input from the target language (Whong, 2011). Motivation, as an aspect of the affective dimension is put forward as one variable that in adults can affect individual achievement. It is argued that for either personal or professional reasons, such motivation can influence second language acquisition, and therefore is an important factor to be considered in pedagogy and curriculum planning (Chomsky, 1988; Stevick, 1990; Dornyei & Ushioda, 2021).

Methods such as community language learning (CLL) (Curran, 1976) counselling-learning (Curran, 1972), suggestapedia (Lozanov, 1978) the silent way (Gattegno, 2010), and total physical response (Asher, 2012) were all informed by the humanistic considerations of their creators, which took into consideration various psychological factors in language instruction for learners and teachers. The emphasis however was on how these various psychological factors shaped the experience of the language classroom for the learner, and indeed in some approaches the teachers also (Curran, 1972). In each of these methods, the learner was not pressured to speak but rather the classroom context and teaching method in producing less stress on the learner encouraged them to take the 'risk' of speaking and making mistakes. Such methods entrusted each learner with the potential to improve learning when they were in a positive emotional state (Larsen-Freeman & Anderson, 2011).

The humanistic aspect of these methods could clearly be applied to both the strong and weak versions of CLT, though they are not necessarily inherent in their procedures. Rather, the social-humanistic skills of the teacher are required to ensure that these concerns are put into place.

The linguistic or language dimension of language learning and teaching can be seen as informing many of the premises behind the broad number of manifestations of the CLT approach that were born during the communicative period (Whong, 2011). While supporting arguments for a debate pedagogy as dialogic and humanistic, they do so indirectly given their rather narrow concern with cognition; which is only one part of the whole learning process (Dufva, 2013; Dornyei & Ryan, 2015; Farid-Arbab, 2016).

Firstly, and perhaps in support of Krashen's more passive conception of SLA in his natural method (2000), it has been established that a good deal of SLA happens incidentally (Whong, 2011, 98). In the context of education, this corresponds to teaching explicit knowledge in a teacher-centred manner from a Synthetic Syllabus, versus that of student-centred Discovery Learning whereby the learner comes across new language as it emerges in context from an Analytic Syllabus. This can be seen in teaching by communicative activities via any of the four skills of reading, listening, speaking and writing in which new vocabulary is either encountered (via the receptive skills) or where a gap is found in attempting to communicate, and the student seeks an explanation about target grammar or vocabulary. Indeed, SLA research suggests that input through the receptive skills of reading and listening – while necessary – is nonetheless processed or learned implicitly. In a related way, the SLA research has established that 'learners come to know more than what they have been exposed to in the input' (Whong, 2011, 100). This consideration is most often exemplified with the learning of grammar, whereby it is argued that learners produce grammatical structures that are not contained in language input; one conclusion being that the brain comes with a Universal Grammar that organizes grammatical constructions as derived from a set of pre-supplied genetic parameters (Hawkins, 2001; White, 2013). There exist however other competing theories of how and to what degree this cognitive capacity draws on more general cognitive abilities (Tomasello, 2003; Halliday & Mathiessen, 2006). Grammatical structures found in learner speech 'often follow predictable paths with predictable stages in the acquisition of a given structure' (Pienneman, 2011, 10). Indeed, processability theory argues that when gaps in learner knowledge are exposed in language lessons, that target grammar and vocabulary should be taught at that point (Kebler, Liebner, & Mansouri, 2011). This argument relates to the same principle whereby the learning and production of grammatical structures do not occur randomly, but rather, occur in a step-by-step manner which is assumed to relate to cognitive constraints on the relative complexity of a given sentential structure or morphological derivation (Piennemann, 2011). Despite the uniformity of second language learning, individual achievement is, however, variable and not all learners reach the same level of competence (Whong, 2011).

Another point of difference or divergence among language learners is that 'second language learning is variable across linguistic subsystems' (Whong, 2011, 107). A learner may achieve a high level of competence in producing accurate and fluent speech at a high level of proficiency but speak with a strong accent. In this case, the level of attainment as far as accurate pronunciation via the phonetic system does not match the higher level of knowledge of grammar and vocabulary. Likewise, the level of language comprehension in reading and listening may be high in a learner, but their ability to speak is much lower. The research also demonstrates that 'there are limits on the effects of frequency on SLA' (Whong, 2011, 111). Given that learning occurs incrementally, time is needed for the assimilation of grammar. In this sense, linguistic knowledge is not – for most learners – declarative knowledge that can be learned by rote or memorization. Rather, a different part of the brain is responsible for calculating of features of a given language which requires time. So, while input is fundamental, there is a limit to the quantity of how much knowledge that can be attained in a given amount of time (Warren, 2013). A further limitation is created by 'the effect of a learner's first language on SLA' (Whong, 2011, 113). To some degree the L1 will contribute in both a positive and negative way to L2 achievement, the claim being that the L1 can lead and mislead the learning of the L2 (Ellis, 2007;

Swan, 2012). This can occur both positively and negatively as evidenced by 'false friends'. These are words that may be similar in phonetic form in the L1 and the L2 but, possess a different meaning. A similar issue can be caused by the mistranslation of grammatical constructions (Swan, 2012).

The penultimate consideration is that 'there are limits on the effects of instruction' (Whong, 2011, 113). In corollary, it is also the case that certain forms of instruction were found to have a more positive effect than others. Overall, while instruction can indeed support the acquisition, 'learners must also utilize other forms of autonomously or incidentally sourced input via both receptive and productive skills' (Whong, 2011, 114). Indeed, the tenth and final major finding is that 'there are limits on the effects of output (learner production) on language acquisition' (Whong, 2011, 116). Traditionally this refers to the role of speaking and writing. It is not enough to just learn via input, but rather a learner must use such knowledge in order to become proficient (Swain, 2005).

The research findings described providing a useful guide for both curriculum and pedagogical planning, providing general guidelines that could inform both a general approach and a more specific teaching method. The extent to which these insights inform language teaching practice and the teaching of speaking more specifically vary, however. With respect to the teaching of an adult speaking in TEFL via debating, a challenge is striking a balance between providing a necessarily student-centred approach which, nonetheless, could potentially benefit learners explicitly through teaching the language associated with effective debating. As has been previously stated, however, the SLA findings also highlight a gap in the additional factors that impact SLA in the classroom, such as affective experience, the social experience and the curriculum as viewed from a thematic perspective. This is interesting, given that much earlier research at the beginning of the CLT era by both Curran (1972) and Freire (1972) did put forth pedagogical approaches which considered how multiple factors impact SLA; also conceived of as holistic pedagogy.

Post-methods era

The post-methods era has arguably been an extension of the communicative era, rather than a dramatic shift as witnessed with that dawn of Communicative. One of the reasons for this is that rather than language teachers employing single methods or approaches, a variety of aspects taken from a variety of methods and approaches have been drawn on by teachers. This can be said to have occurred as a result of the diverging methods where no single one was taken to offer the single most effective method (Whong, 2011).

The communicative approach to teaching language is still the dominant one in the post-methods era, and as such, this represents a continuation of the eschewing of the traditional grammar-translation methods and the artificial, less authentic approaches to teaching speaking found in the earlier periods discussed. Attention is paid to more learner-centred authentic communication, and personal relevance of topics and tasks are also common to the approaches found in this present era (Richards & Rodgers, 2014).

Task-based learning (TBL)

TBL is student-centred like some stronger versions of CLT, with the task itself providing the stages of the lesson. This would be in contrast to some of the methods such as the audiolingual method in which the teacher retains control over what the students say and when they say it, as drills of students repeating phrases in unison occur – and are typical of teacher-led classroom communication. TBL centres on the completion of a single task, based on authentic language, adaptable to different contexts depending on aims. It is not based on a grammar syllabus and may centre around a text which serves as a source of new language, requires communication in order to complete the task, and where learners must be fully engaged and through this, use and process the language which drives acquisition (Ellis, 2003; Whong, 2011).

TBL Teaching – as with some of the later approaches and methods discussed – has been informed by SLA research, and is based on five of the broader findings that inform SLA in its application to language teaching: Firstly, that language can be learned best through communication via authentic, real-world oracy. This research has been referred to as the output hypothesis which states that language use drives the acquisition of language (Willis & Willis, 2007). This reflexive input-output dynamic is therefore highly student-centred, with the teacher very much facilitating learning. TBL is also informed by insights from psychological research in SLA, as tasks draw on problem-solving attention, memory and personal interest. Engagement of these resources drives acquisition and entails that acquisition, as these aspects of learner psychology are activated (Whong, 2011). One aspect of the social dimension of language acquisition emphasizes it as a social process, dovetailing with the input-output dynamic. As other more knowledgeable speakers speak, their fellow learners receive this language as input, thus potentially learning a new language, appropriate to the task. Learners may therefore support and scaffold lower-level learners throughout the task (Van den Branden, 2006).

Debating can be seen to afford these ways of language learning insights, based on the various practices associated with it, and its apparent affordances for the language learner as outlined so far as a form of dialogic speaking.

The lexical approach

The lexical approach has been informed by developments in the study of syntax and lexical acquisition in both first and second language learners and is also based – like TBL – on learning situated language in context (Whong, 2011). The proposals of these theories as found in word grammar and construction grammar are cognitive linguistic theories of SLA, in which there are dependencies between words and phrases (Goldberg, 1995; Hudson, 2010). This is in contrast to the structural constituency approach found in Chomskyan grammar of languages, such as in the current Minimalist program (Edelstein, 2020). What this means for SLA and language teaching is the belief that we learn about the lexical properties of words as they cluster into phrases and collocations between words and phrases (Lewis, 1993). One example of this might be found in the learning of the phrasal verb 'participate in'. This verb phrase – for it to form a complete clause must be either complemented by a preceding subject noun phrase or an object noun phrase. The challenge for a second language learner in correctly formulating this clause, however, is not found in the more complex overall syntactic formulation of the sentence, but in the selection of the correct preposition 'in', instead of 'to'. With this knowledge, the lexical approach would therefore aim to teach this particular verb-particle phrase, knowing that it is of greater difficulty to acquire. The lexical approach proposes that the presentation of this target language be provided as input in context, such as in the study of an article that features authentic language that includes these target terms. The approach can be applied to the teaching of writing and speaking in context, in addition to separate exercises that focus on the explicit study of the language (Willis & Willis, 2007).

In this way, dialogic speaking and debating may be complementary methods that could adopt a focus on studying language in context, given that particular topics require a focus on particularly vocabulary, and the language of argumentation a similarly, relatively predictable range of grammar.

The role of new technologies as new methods

Technology has played an increasing role in how teaching methods are being applied, in particular as a consequence of the Covid pandemic where a large amount of English language teaching was transferred to online, exploiting the internet as a medium (González-Lloret et al., 2021; Li et al., 2021). There is ongoing research into student experiences of online teaching, with the role of both dialogic teaching and the affective dimension continuing to be of relevance in this new learning environment. One question about this sea change relates to the experience of teaching and learning to speak online, an area of research that is still in its early stages due to the very recent occurrence of this phenomenon.

While during the 1980s and 1990s, receptive skills such as listening were enhanced by tape recorders, this has since been supplanted by compact discs and then MP3s which could be accessed via websites online, with the internet offering an array of possibilities for complete self-supported autonomous listening lessons. The proliferation of mobile phones with internet access has also significantly improved opportunities for learners to engage in language lessons and exercises (Larsen-Freeman & Anderson, 2011). In very recent times, Artificial Intelligence has been utilized as a way of offering personalized learning to learners. All of this progress has led to more efficient and potentially more effective ways in which learners may practice language skills, and language systems ranging from pronunciation, grammar and vocabulary (Kessler, 2018). This new direction, however, shows signs of leading to a preference for one-to-one learning between teacher and student, which would limit the nature of dialogue at least as far as goes the variety of input from fellow learners is concerned. Nonetheless, from the affective perspective, one-to-one teaching – depending on the learner – could well offer a number of important benefits, i.e. the possibility of personalization entails learner choice, and also the possibility for the teacher to adapt to the specific needs of the learner, rather than compromise through the often-needed amount of differentiation typical of larger groups (Liu, 2018).

Chapter summary

Initially, the evolution of TEFL was driven by the changing social needs of Westerners, and not on the basis of scientific research. It was driven by the need of people to communicate with each other across regions of the world, where previously they experienced a form of separation due to their linguistic differences. And when the third era, which was informed by science, took place it was later superseded once again by the social needs of learners. From this perspective, it is interesting that the social dimension and its fuller implications for a second language have been still rather marginalized, and that the affective experience of the social dimension – an undeniable and inseparable aspect of social experience – is even more so. The current situation, however, shows signs of continual evolution towards greater recognition of their role to support English language teaching.

Speaking in TEFL is a phenomenon that is key in developing a foreign language for a multitude of reasons, and this has given way to the current paradigm of communicative language teaching and learning. Despite its inception, some fifty years ago in the 1970s, large-scale research has recently found that globally, speaking persists as by far the biggest challenge facing students and teachers.

3

A Brief History of Debating

The origin of debating as a form of dialogic speech in the historical record can be seen to have been founded and to have evolved over thousands of years. Its history can most clearly be understood as an unravelling of human advancement across time, through the successive nature of progressive religious dispensations from Hinduism, some 5,000 years ago, up to the most recent world religion, the Baha'i faith (Momen, 1999). Dialogic practices appear, therefore, to be situated in moments in which new spiritual teachings are brought forth in each age, from the East to the West. The following section will survey some of the origins and practices of debating – in order of when the religion arrived – as a form of progressive revelation that is of note due to their contribution to dialogue as a means towards the achievement of human progress in the arts and the sciences.

Dialogue has played an important role in the history of Hinduism, which is believed to be the world's oldest religion that gave birth to a broad set of cultural practices and developments in the Far East. Dialogue has been one such communicative practice that came from such developments. The Vedas which can be traced back to the beginnings of Hinduism contain ancient scriptures which themselves were created through dialogic speaking between seers and sages of the time. The tradition can be seen to have been continued by the Upanishads, which represent a Hindu philosophy related to the individual and the nature of the universe, alongside other aspects of philosophy such as ontology and epistemology. The composition of such texts was based on discussion between teacher and student, debating various topics (Klostermaier, 2007; Fowler, 2012). The Bhagavad Gita is perhaps the most well known of Hindu texts, and indeed perhaps the most circulated, globally. It is structured along the lines of a debate between a warrior and Krishna, as Krishna teaches and guides the warrior Arjuna, in his learning about spiritual philosophy (Eknath, 2019).

Hindu culture has also been influenced over time through interaction and dialogue within the faith. For example, the Advaita Vedanta school emphasizes a view of reality that is non-dualist and came about as a result of interreligious dialogue between Hindus and Buddhists. Elsewhere, the Charaka Samhita is a Sanskrit text on the Ayurvedic approach to medicine where there is a section that discusses the logic of debating (Sharma, 2014). Even nowadays, dialogue can be considered to play a part in Hinduism when it is employed for interfaith dialogue where issues of politics and academics continue to be discussed. It is quite evident that dialogic communication – in the form of debate – has played a crucial role in the development and continued existence of Hindu culture, spirituality and intellectual traditions, and has done so over many thousands of years (Ram-Prasad, 2007; Jindal, 2017).

In Jewish history, debating has also been a cornerstone of dialogic practices, as can be seen in the Talmud – an ancient compilation of discussions and commentaries related to Jewish law and philosophy. Many of the discussions had a practical impact on Jewish life, influencing communities throughout the world in different ways (Cohen, 2009). Jewish intellectual practices continually and rigorously debate various aspects of this inheritance, related to religion, philosophy and the law (Fox, 2008). During the medieval period, the act of debating held an important place in Jewish history, taking place in public forums, such as the disputations between Jewish scholars and Christian theologians that were common in Europe during the Middle Ages. The debates were high stakes, with Jewish scholars not only engaging in intellectual enquiry but also defending Judaism and Jewish beliefs against Christian attacks (Katz, 2006). In more recent times, Jewish debating has evolved into a more academic and intellectual pursuit, with scholars engaging in debates and discussions about Jewish philosophy, ethics and law. The establishment of yeshivas, Jewish religious schools, during the nineteenth and twentieth centuries, has provided Jewish scholars with a forum to engage in debates and discussions about Jewish law and tradition (Berger, 1996). Jewish debating continues to play a central role in Jewish intellectual life, with Jewish scholars and students partaking in discussions about a broad number of subjects, ranging from the interpretation of Jewish texts to contemporary ethical issues. Debating societies and clubs are also common in Jewish schools and universities, encouraging students to develop their critical thinking and public speaking skills, whilst engaging with Jewish ideas and tradition (Schechter, 2018).

The renowned ancient Greek philosophers Socrates, Plato and Aristotle are depicted as being constantly engaged in debate, with their dialogic practices being reflected in the style of communication that many of their works illustrate. Indeed, such practices were part of their tradition and their debating skills. While each of these philosophers held their own precise beliefs, they nonetheless arrived at a series of distinct and lasting material and spiritual truths, and attitudes towards a wide-ranging number of issues in philosophy (Oaklander, 2014). It has been claimed that Socrates, who lived in Athens during the fifth century BCE, was influenced by his travels to ancient Israel, by Jewish Rabbis (Baha'u'llah, 1993; Abdul Baha, 2011). He is known for his method of debate, which has since been termed 'Socratic questioning': with this approach, he would engage his interlocutors with a series of logical questions that would often challenge them, and lead to new ways of seeing, some of which were highly controversial for the time; for example, his belief in a monotheistic God, during a period when there were believed to be multiple deities (Abdul Baha, 2011). Socrates' dialogue can be considered as a dialectic method that was employed in order to arrive at logical conclusions that were clear and rigorous, as he taught that this was a reliable way in which to discover the truth. Instead of expressing mere opinions, his interest and style of teaching sought to uncover hard facts about truth and indeed the limitations of human knowledge. Plato, who further developed Greek philosophy in the footsteps of his teacher Socrates, employed the dialectic method, by presenting complex arguments which often featured Socrates. This approach to verbal communication as found in his writings, covered topics such as the definition of justice and a number of important theories related to ontology (Plato & Waterfield, 2008). Aristotle's approach to debating differed in so far as he placed an even greater emphasis on logical argumentation and empirical observation, still however employing a dialectical approach. Aristotle believed that the most effective debates were those that involved an objective analysis of the facts, and emphasized the importance of empirical evidence and reasoning in arriving at conclusions (Aristotle, 2023). Throughout the ancient world, debating played a key role in political and intellectual life, as engagement in discussions and arguments to explore important questions was found to be a means of arriving at important conclusions to both issues of the time and what were also considered to be eternal truths. Greek philosophy can therefore be seen to have developed as a means of communicating – that while its conclusions might not always be popular – still have the potential to act as a powerful and efficacious method and approach to learning (Evangelidis, 2016).

 The arrival of Buddhism further developed its own traditions of debating, which had an expressly spiritual purpose. The Buddha himself is said to have encouraged his disciples to question and seek out truth through a process of debating. The purposes remain the same as those of Hindu and Jewish traditions that came before, whereby, as was found in the later developments that occurred during the progress accomplished by the Greeks, philosophical truths were sought about the nature of reality (Perdue, 1992). Early Buddhist communities utilized debate as a means of resolving conflicts and clarifying the meaning of Buddhist teachings. Monks and laypeople discussed and debated various aspects of Buddhist philosophy, including topics such as the nature of suffering, the nature of the self and the path to enlightenment (Buswell, 2004). The spread of Buddhism led to the development of intellectual thought, being employed in Buddhist monasteries as a part of the pedagogical approach to education, and covered a broad number of important issues. One such approach involves a Buddhist monk being challenged to provide the answer to a question: the process involves a series of symbolic spiritual gestures that express acceptance or rejection of the monk's teaching. The physical actions acted out reflect a process of growth and rebirth in which the challenger's original position – if defeated – symbolically disposes of the erroneous thinking, thus enabling a forward movement towards a new level of spirituality (Perdue, 1992). In recent years, Buddhist debating has continued, both in traditional Buddhist communities and in modern contexts. In many Buddhist countries, debating competitions and festivals are still held, and in some cases, have become major cultural events. In addition, online forums and social media have provided new opportunities for Buddhists from around the world to engage in philosophical debates and discussions (Ray, 2018). The Buddhist employment of debating can therefore be seen to provide a model which is also inspired as a form of education that seeks to achieve progress through a natural philosophy and a spiritual philosophy, so as to improve a collective social understanding of the nature of society and human progress (Gethin, 1998).

The history of Christianity as a religion also clearly demonstrates how debating has shaped and formed its evolution and continued new directions, as was particularly made clear during the Reformation. Increasingly informed by philosophical thinking that came from the Greeks, Catholicism evolved as the centuries went by. Indeed, after the enormous consequences of the Reformation, both Protestants and Catholics alike have sought to continually analyse and determine their similarities and differences (Olson, 2011). Debates have also taken place between Christians and other religions, in particular with Jews and Muslims. Thomas Aquinas is one such Catholic Christian philosopher who is still cited as representing an approach to intellectual thought – not limited to topics of Christianity. His approach to logic and argument represents a style of debate which is still cited and practised (Feser, 2009). Such debating often takes place in university settings among academics, and yet also by pastors and priests within the ever-increasing social media environments where many complex debates continue (Noll & Nystrom, 2016). In sum, Christianity has drawn on debating as a means of intellectual enquiry providing a detailed discussion about the reasoning behind truths that the church holds about the role of Christianity in society (Noll & Nystrom, 2016).

The advent of Islam which came about some 600 years after the birth of Christianity brought about a number of significant strides forward in science and intellectual progress. Muslims are encouraged to accept other believers of monotheistic faiths and engage in dialogue as a means of promoting peace and mutual understanding among all of the previous religions outlined in the Quran that are said to have come from God (Khan et al., 2020). This is also evidenced in the continued engagement of Islamic scholars to debate various topics contained within the Quran that concern theological differences that are maintained by other religions. Within the Islamic world, laws and practices have developed across regions in which Islam still dominates. In modern times, debates have continued regarding the clash of modernity with some of what have been perceived to be strict rules and laws concerning, for example, women's rights and human rights. The treatment of these issues, however, may differ from country to country (Küçük, 2016). Nonetheless, Islamic history can be seen to have made significant contributions through openness to intellectual enquiry, rigorous scholarship and ongoing debates with both other religions and secular traditions worldwide (Kerns, 2014).

Dialogue, termed 'consultation' is a cornerstone of the newest world religion – the Baha'i faith. Dialogue is explicitly taught as a way of democratically seeking truth before taking action on a given issue. The Baha'i faith's teachings make clear the fundamental necessity of believers consulting together as a means of advancing their cause, which entails the progress of humanity into a new era whereby clerical authority has been replaced with the dialogic style of democratic consultation (Spaces of Consultation, n.d.). The practice of consultation occurs within study circles and spiritual assemblies whose members are voted for by believers to carry out the duties of being involved with the teaching work and other issues that Baha'i communities manage through their approach to serving their neighbourhoods and cities. The faith is also involved with interreligious groups that seek to foster harmonious relationships between people of all faiths, as they maintain that all religions come from God. The Baha'is also invite the public to participate in 'meaningful conversations' whereby people can freely discuss their attitudes and beliefs. These groups are intended to provide a service to people who are searching for answers to important contemporary topics and are encouraged to discuss them (Meaningful and Distinctive Conversations, 2013). The Baha'i approach to dialogue can therefore be seen as an explicit means of seeking truth, and guidelines as to how Baha'is comport in such contexts are fully supported by Baha'i teachings. This general approach has as its chief aim the betterment of the world through building positive collaborative communities (Kolstoe, 1985).

Debating as teaching speaking in EFL

The historical role that debating as a form of dialogic communication has had demonstrates that its role has been chiefly educational, i.e. to drive the teaching of students and the education of scholars, and teachers. As a communicational form, it is therefore not surprising that during what is essentially still a communicative era in language teaching, debating would be found to serve as an appropriate method of learning content knowledge via a second language, and in this process learning both incidentally and explicitly the target language.

In the previous chapters, the importance of speaking as dialogue in language learning has been highlighted (Aclan & Aziz, 2015) as a way of improving cognitive goals such as vocabulary, communicative goals such as increased conversation and discussion (Al-ikhani & Bagheridoust, 2017), social goals such as increased engagement (Al-Ghamdi et al., 2019), educational goals such as improved relevance of content and critical thinking (Elhassan & Adam, 2017) and the humanistic goal of improved experience of EFL classes (Akerman & Neale, 2011).

Historically, the purposes of debating can be seen as having fulfilled a didactic, dialectical and dialogic role; furthermore, at times, such communication might have competitive tendencies (Rybold & Harvey-Smith, 2013). On the other hand, debate has clearly been employed to share knowledge and teach through an exchange of ideas (Elhassan & Adam, 2017). In this way, it might be surprising that debate as a communicative method in language teaching – in the broader sense – plays such a small part in educational practice, given its long history and importance as a method of educating humankind for thousands of years. When considered in relation to second language learning, and the importance of interaction through both listening and speaking – it is perhaps even more surprising that employing debate as the central part of pedagogy and curriculum is so absent in ELT (Akerman & Neale, 2011). Indeed, the use of debating as a way of teaching English as a foreign or second language (ESL/EFL) has a relatively recent history (Akerman & Neale, 2011). Over the years, the use of debating in ESL/EFL classrooms has become increasingly popular, with many educators recognizing its value as a way to engage students in the language learning process and to promote the development of higher-order thinking skills. Debating is seen as a way to encourage students to express themselves in English, develop their ability to argue and defend their ideas and improve their overall fluency and confidence in using the language (Iman, 2017). Debating is used in a variety of different ESL/EFL settings, from schools to universities, and is often integrated into the curriculum as a way to enhance language learning outcomes. Debating can take many different forms, from informal classroom discussions to more formal debates with structured rules and procedures (Aclan & Aziz, 2015).

Debating requires the student to consider a topic or an issue, gain a thorough knowledge of it, and then express their position in a logical, clear and coherent manner (Freely & Steinberg, 2014). The practice is also usually based on a topic of interest arbitrated by a panel or chair (Snider & Schnurer, 2006). Where it is most often found employed as an extra-curricular competitive activity (Akerman & Neale, 2011), it is also employed as a form of pedagogy. One of the most significant developments in the use of debating in ESL/EFL classrooms has been the emergence of international debating competitions and tournaments. These events bring together students from around the world to compete in English language debates on a wide range of topics, providing an opportunity for students to develop their language skills, interact with students from different cultures, and learn more about global issues (Rybold & Harvey-Smith, 2013). However, this approach takes on a competitive character and therefore represents just one approach.

Contemporary perspectives

While a good deal of studies into the efficacy of debating in native-speaking studies has been done, only a small number of studies have demonstrated how debates have been used in foreign language education to great effect, though much more research is needed to explore its affordances (Akerman and Neale, 2011). Thus far, however, it is reported that 'student perception data indicates that engaging in debate activities increases engagement' (Akerman & Neale, 2011, 18), and debates have been shown to improve the communicative skills of participants (Colbert, 1995; Akerman & Neale, 2011, 20). Additionally, debating as a communicative task has also been found to be meaningful, and authentic, as it engages learner experiences and points of view. This is in comparison with more traditional grammar-translation models, which are focused on the topics and texts provided by the teacher (Aclan & Aziz, 2015). It is also argued that in a continually globalized world reform of communication practices in EFL and language teaching still requires moving from a traditional teacher-centred model to a dialogue-based approach, and debating is one such method suited to this (Inoue & Nakano, 2004 in Akerman & Neale, 2011, 16). Social and humanistic benefits such as increased confidence, self-esteem and broadening horizons – though not in relation to any language teaching research specifically – have also been demonstrated as affordances of debating in EFL (Akerman & Neale, 2011).

Interestingly, it is in the work of humanistic scholars, who appeared during the advent of the communicative period – such as Curran (1972), but particularly Freire (1974) – that debate was first conceived as a fundamental language teaching method (Freire, 1972). In terms of the actual application of debating as a task spread across a series of lessons, or more simply as a one-off communicative activity, it is difficult to ascertain to what extent debating is employed as an activity in EFL or ESOL. Two of the major handbooks on English language teaching such as Harmer (2013) and Scrivener (2005) do recommend speaking discussion activities but do not use the term 'debate'. One weakness here is that such activities are not exploited for their significant potential to make connections to developing other skills. The skill of reading, for example, could be incorporated into the pre-debate research stage as evidenced in my research and elsewhere (Akerman & Neale, 2011). Looking back at the articles cited, debating is a form of speaking that is mainly argued for in Eastern foreign language contexts, and within those contexts, it is claimed to be a new and innovative method of teaching speaking (Aclan & Aziz, 2015).

That such comprehensive research into debating in TEFL is lacking is perhaps indexical to the many questions and debates about the nature of language acquisition from a holistic viewpoint. What these dimensions that have been neglected could indicate is that Scientism continues to lead the way in studies into second language acquisition and language teaching research (Dufva, 2013). A combination of research into both the cognitive and the affective which enquires into the learner's experience of learning could provide a holistic perspective, thus informing teacher practice and improving learner outcomes. As a research method, this was also the one employed by Curran (1972) and Freire (1974) and on which they formulated their humanistic-orientated pedagogy and theories of education which this book draws.

Chapter summary

Successful language learning – when it takes place in a social context – occurs when individuals collaborate instead of compete, an increasingly popular position in educational practice and research. In this sense, it has a moral and ethical dimension which is foundational, if the goals of successful SLA are the main aim of such education and educational research. And yet, the initiatives of social and emotional learning (SEL) which can be considered to be a move towards these goals are only emerging. The 'debates' that have ensued in North America surrounding this issue themselves resemble an absolutist political conflict of diverging ideologies – as opposed to a progressive form of dialogue.

The point here is that debating as a form of human verbal communication has a long pedigree – and in its best form – is in harmony with traditions of human communication which can be traced through history to show a gradual progress in the ability and achievements of peoples to move forward intellectually and morally in their behaviour and in their evolving ideals – which form the bedrock of progressive societies.

4

Dialogic Teaching and Second Language Acquisition

Introduction

This chapter is divided into four main sections: The first foundational section surveys the main findings from second language acquisition research and their implications for language teaching on the whole. This is done so as to situate the second section on the teaching of speaking in contemporary TEFL to adults, which is the main language skill associated with the study. These two initial foundations support the main two pillars of the research which are those of debating as a form of dialogic teaching in section three, followed by how dialogic – and more specifically given the focus of the study – speaking can be seen to promote a form of humanistic pedagogy in the final fourth section.

The review seeks to highlight the underrepresentation of research into learner experience of speaking lessons, and how existing research, and that of the initial promotors of teaching dialogic speaking as humanistic pedagogy, provide insights and a direction in which a dialogic approach to curriculum and pedagogical design using debating could ameliorate some of the current issues.

Contemporary findings from second language acquisition research and their implications for language teaching

The following findings mainly reflect the prioritization of the linguistic or language dimension of language learning and teaching and can be seen as informing many of the premises behind the broad number of manifestations of the CLT approach that were born during the communicative period (Whong, 2011). While some of these findings do support arguments for a debate pedagogy as dialogic and humanistic, they do so indirectly given their rather narrow concern with cognition; which is only one part of the whole learning process (Dufva, 2013).

The penultimate consideration is that 'there are limits on the effects of instruction' (Whong, 2011, 113). In corollary, it is also the case that certain forms of instruction are found to have a more positive effect than others. Overall, while instruction can indeed support the acquisition, 'learners must also utilize other forms of autonomously or incidentally sourced input via both receptive and product skills' (Whong, 2011, 114). Indeed, the tenth and final major finding is that 'there are limits on the effects of output (learner production) on language acquisition' (Whong, 2011, 116). Traditionally this refers to the role of speaking and writing. It is not enough to just learn via speaking and writing, but rather a learner must receive input in order to become proficient, or indeed to make any progress at all (Swain, 2005).

The research findings described provide a useful guide for both curriculum and pedagogical planning, as guidelines that could inform both a general approach and a more specific teaching method. The extent to which these insights inform language teaching practice and the teaching of speaking more specifically vary, however. With respect to the teaching of adult speaking in TEFL via debating, a challenge is striking a balance between providing a necessarily student-centred approach which – nonetheless – could potentially benefit learners, through explicitly teaching the language associated with effective debating. As has been previously stated, however, the SLA findings also highlight a gap in the additional factors that impact SLA in the classroom, such as affective experience, the social experience and the curriculum as viewed from a thematic perspective. This is interesting, given that much earlier research at the beginning of the CLT era by both Curran (1972) and Freire (1972) did put forth pedagogical approaches which considered how multiple factors impact SLA.

Cultural historical theory and language teaching

One popular theory of language learning also offers an account of SLA that incorporates the findings of broader SLA research discussed, but that has recently expanded to complement the approaches to SLA and language teaching from psychology that addresses the subjective dimension which this book argues for is cultural historical theory (CHT) (or 'cultural historical psychology').

Cultural historical psychological theory (CHPT) is one of the few overall theories of learning that potentially encompasses the most comprehensive overview and explanation of SLA and instruction, which has been drawn on by some second language researchers – and has been argued as a promising approach given its scope (Lantolf & Thorne, 2006). The theory accounts for children's and adults' learning in formal education at the internal cognitive level and the external socio-cultural historical level; both areas which this book holds to determine language learning outcomes. Despite this apparently comprehensive approach that has certainly been found support through research and practice (Lantolf & Thorne, 2006), it has only in recent years, been put into question by CHP scholars who have identified its undeveloped attention to the role of subjective experience; i.e. psychological factors such as emotion, personality and *perezhvanie*. This previous deficit, however, and its subsequent arguments pertaining to its revision, can be seen to complement the growing calls from positive psychology within SLA to inform SLA theory.

The term 'perezhivanie', a Russian word employed by Vygotsky and his contemporaries, is understood in cultural historical theory to have a number of functions, of which the following two could be pertinent to researching the experiential dimension of education: perezhivanie, according to Rubenstein is 'that which proves to be personally significant', and for Leontyev, 'emotional perezhivanie are manifested as internal signals, by means of which are realized the personal sense of an event' (Meshcheryakova, 2016). These definitions of perezhivanie as an expression of subjective experience can be seen to represent the part of our consciousness that enables us, potentially to reflect on emotional experience, and is, therefore, an important concept and function when considering educational experiences. Dewey – at around the same time as Vygotsky stated that 'everything (in education) depends upon the quality of the experience which is had' (Dewey, 1938). Dewey's assertion was that as far as an evaluation of the various, though diverging merits of traditional versus progressive models of education – primarily – they should be concerned with the experience of education; therefore, it is to these experiences that the attention will now be drawn.

The role of experience which comprises subjectivity – according to these recent developments in CHT is fundamental to one's 'sense of self' as a social being acting in cultural and historical contexts. That is to say that the cultural and social dimensions are said to shape the individual's experiences – which includes the whole range of psychological aspects of experience including emotion and the other array of psychological factors that are examined in SLA research (Gonzalez-Rey et al., 2019). This complements the more developed aspects of Vygotskian theory that emphasize the dynamics of cognitive development, as the external social plane stimulates and informs the internal plane of mind. The individual, however, possesses the ability to actively construct knowledge through partaking in educational processes: this is mediated via artefacts such as technological tools and social interaction (Vygotsky, 1978; Lantolf & Thorne, 2006). These new developments that focus on subjectivity argue that personal experience and perception do indeed influence learning (Busygina & Yaroshevskaya, 2020). This is an important dimension for second or other language learners, given the significant and unique challenges associated with the psychological aspects of SLA for language learners and teachers (Dornyei & Ryan, 2015).

These recent developments in CHPT that bring up to date the role of subjectivity in the theory, therefore, catch up with earlier advances outside of CHT that emerged since the CLT period began as have been described earlier in relation to the history of English language teaching. To restate, the rationale for its inclusion in this discussion regarding SLA and teaching is its comprehensive nature as a single theory of learning which could address the broad aspects of SLA which are contingent on the subjective and the social.

The current teaching of speaking

Contemporary practice, informed by SLA research in TEFL is categorized based on the dichotomy of the various formulations of CLT that are said to be manifested across a scale of its stronger and weaker forms (Howatt & Smith, 2014). The stronger forms include dialogic speaking as a form of pedagogy, yet also address how curriculum design can be built on interactive, dialogic consultation with students.

An example of the weaker version of CLT would be when a range of short communicative activities are drawn on from a textbook in a language class, an example being, a short listening comprehension task, followed by a brief discussion of a topic in which students share their experiences or points of view. The following lesson might then emphasize a different language skill or attention to a different language system (grammar) or vocabulary. This is often organized according to a grammar syllabus, however, in which target grammatical forms and vocabulary related to a specific topic are practised. Attention is also often paid to written grammar exercises that reflect structuralist linguistic methods from the scientific period, often focused on grammar. In its stronger form, CLT as manifested in Thornbury and Meddings' Teaching Unplugged approach

(2010) – student's experiences and perspectives are the 'texts' or source of input; the method affords an increased personal and deeper engagement compared to the weaker form of CLT. A teacher may use a whiteboard or blackboard to build up a text based on the experiences and opinions of the participants, derived from a series of connected speaking tasks related to one topic. This is in contrast to a textbook-based pedagogy that may concern itself more with a broad topic that invites learners to discuss their experiences and opinions to a more limited degree and focuses more on comprehension of the content of the book. Thornbury and Meddings (2010) have argued that such content can be found in the contributions that the participants have to offer and that a language syllabus be derived from the missing grammar and vocabulary that students do not yet know as they grapple with trying to communicate. Only at that point, and usually at the end of a lesson is grammar or vocabulary taught explicitly. Thornbury terms this structuring of a language lesson as offering explicit teaching of grammar and vocabulary at the point of need. In contrast to Krashen's emphasis on learning a new language via exposure to input, Thornbury and Meddings emphasize the role of output. Nonetheless, however, both approaches address the concern of how a new language can be learned.

The syllabus proposed by Thornbury and Meddings reflects Wilkins' conception of an Analytic Syllabus, which is contrasted with the aforementioned weak form of CLT syllabus (Larsen-Freeman & Anderson, 201)1. This approach can be seen to be far more dynamic than that of a pre-planned language syllabus that can only make general assumptions about what language is needed for a group of learners at a given point in their language-learning journey. Of course, this approach could be more appropriate when students are being prepared for an exam in which there is a specific language syllabus on which they will be tested. The issue however that such an approach presents is in the assumption that learners learn what they are taught regardless of their current level of acquisition. This is not the case though, with research showing that acquisition only takes place when a learner is at the appropriate stage of their 'interlanguage' (foreign language) development (Kebler, Liebner, & Mansouri, 2011).

This brief survey captures the main divergent approaches of the weak and strong versions of CLT, with the exception of TBL. TBL also reflects the division between methods that utilize a strong communicative approach and is based on an Analytic Syllabus. SLA research supports the use of such syllabi as previously highlighted by Krashen's input hypothesis (1983) and Pienneman's processability theory (Kebler, Liebner, & Mansouri, 2011). TBL provides a clearly staged meaningful process wherein students are given a task that they must complete. This could be planning the itinerary for a trip or researching new information for a presentation. In this process, their comprehension skills are tested and new gaps in language knowledge are potentially discovered. Both students and teachers are provided with a clear overview of language gaps which can be meaningfully taught as they emerge (Ellis, 2003; Nunan, 2004). This method is very similar to Thornbury and Meddings' (2010) Teaching Unplugged in its rationale, the only difference being that their approach is not based on functional tasks necessarily but rather discussions about experience or opinions.

As it was initially conceived, and according to the likes of both Curran (1972) and Freire (1974), from the perspective of humanism the stronger the version of CLT that is taught the more its humanistic potential is. The basic rationale is that the more the curriculum enables the learner to engage in topics of interest and a pedagogy that allows them to express themselves through speaking, the greater the potential to learn. As such, dialogic speaking can be contrasted with non-dialogic as witnessed in the weaker forms of CLT as potentially less humanistic.

The role of the English language teacher

The above findings in a general manner inform the design of the current state of English language teacher training. Therefore, given that there is a benchmark entry-level qualification for English language teachers which is accepted in most of the world, it seems appropriate to be aware from the outset of how it currently defines and assesses successful teaching. While the following assessment criteria are broad, they are nonetheless useful for situating and supporting an understanding of the theory and practice of language teaching, with an emphasis on the teaching of speaking. As with the SLA research however, the following teaching practice policy can be seen to downplay and underspecify the factors that at the beginning of the CLT era were argued to impact on second language learning education.

While the origin of the aforementioned qualification and its assessment criteria were formed by International House, an international English language teaching franchise, some years ago Cambridge University's English language teaching and

Table 1 Teacher assessment overview

1.	Assess learner needs, and plan and teach lessons that take account of learners' backgrounds, learning preferences and current needs.
2.	Demonstrate language knowledge and awareness, and appropriate teaching strategies.
3.	Demonstrate knowledge about language skills and how they may be acquired.
4.	Plan and prepare lessons designed to develop their learners' overall language competence.
5.	Demonstrate an appropriate range of teaching skills at this level and show professional awareness and responsibility.

(Cambridge English, 2021, 2) (Table 1. Cambridge CELTA teacher criteria)

assessment took it over. The organization has continued to set the standard for English schools in their recruitment of new teachers, requiring the Certificate in English language teaching to Adults as an entry-level qualification. This combines with their extensive textbook ranges for teachers which can be seen to provide the basis of a general pedagogy for English teachers teaching exam candidates. Cambridge English also owns and manages the dominant English language qualifications for students, through Cambridge English Assessment designs, publishes and assesses Cambridge English exams. Due to this dominance, and their following of the agreed European common language learning framework, the below assessment standards are taken to be a potentially significant framework. Lastly, the Cambridge exams feature a speaking task in which two or three candidates are expected to discuss a topic in a manner that is representative of the basic requisites involved in a debate. As such, speaking tasks of the same nature are present in Cambridge language teaching textbooks, and therefore it is possible that a teacher would facilitate a lesson based on discussion-debating on which the below criteria (see Table 1) would be applied in assessing a trainee teacher.

The criteria will not form the main basis of the Discussion chapter, as other more appropriate approaches to language pedagogy provide a more detailed explanatory account that better informs debating as a humanistic pedagogy and therefore more with my philosophy of education. Some consideration, however, of these broad concerns will be included where relevant. With respect to the more specific aims of teaching speaking in TEFL, the following section will describe how the more general developments in ELT research apply to the practice of teaching speaking.

Speaking in language teaching practice in TEFL

The aforementioned history of EFL and ESOL showed how the second of the main four major periods started what has continued to be a more widespread acceptance that learning to speak is fundamental in successful language acquisition (Howatt & Smith, 2014). Both the third scientific period (1920–70), informed by Behaviourism, then the current communicative period (1970–2000+) which was informed by insights from both formal linguistics and sociolinguistics continued the emphasis on speaking as a skill, but via different methodological approaches and methods (Larsen-Freeman, 2011). Most significantly, the CLT era introduced the significance of humanistic considerations as part of an increasingly holistic approach to education. This has chiefly been argued for in relation to the teaching of dialogic speaking as initially argued for by Freire (1972) in language education, and more broadly in education by Alexander (2020).

Some of the early approaches which emphasized speaking during the CLT period, from the beginning of that era in the 1970s were also humanistic methods, and have since been termed 'designer approaches' due to their specific philosophy and methods. These designer approaches are said to have influenced what has since become a broader communicative teaching practice due to the move towards a greater student-centred approach to teaching (Whong, 2011). This is evidenced also in the basic entry-level language teacher training (Cambridge, 2021) in which humanistic considerations are taught, though not in a manner specific to any one of the early designer methods (Cambridge, 2021). The connection between CLT, freer speaking and dialogic speaking, and humanism were made early on by Curran (1972) and Freire (1972) and as has been outlined in SLA research informing language teaching are still held to be guiding principles for informing teaching practice (Arnold, 2011; Cambridge, 2021). Certainly, International House (International House, 2021), Bell Education (Bell, 2021), Inlingua (Inlingua, 2021) and Wall Street (Wall Street English, n.d.) – four of the largest and most widespread private English language schools for adults – base their teaching methods on the weak to strong communicative scale. While Berlitz-type schools still teach speaking using the audiolingual method from the scientific period, few schools continue to draw on these earlier methods (Larsen-Freeman & Anderson, 2011), thus supporting the efficacy claimed by Curran and Freire at the beginning of the current paradigm of CLT for dialogic speaking, due to its potential to unify speaking as communication with the other crucial factors of education (as curriculum): the social and cognition (Curran, 1972; Freire, 1974).

Contemporary research into teaching adult EFL speaking

The following literature highlights the significance and importance of a dialogic approach to the teaching of speaking to adults, in contrast with a non-dialogical approach, which is considered a weak form of CLT speaking at best, or a grammar-translation method when it is furthest from it. Its import is found to rest on the necessity for students to be given the opportunity for 'output' as it is conceived in SLA research (Whong, 2011) or expression, liberation and sharing in the holistic approaches such as found in Curran (1972) and Freire (1974).

Despite Curran and Freire's contributions to the CLT era as outlined previously, it has been claimed that much research into the teaching of speaking in adult EFL represents the dominant concerns within linguistics that inform language teaching, whereas the social and affective dimensions which are representative of a more holistic approach to second language acquisition and teaching have been absent in prior decades (Dufva, 2013), and only recently taken up in growing numbers (Dewaele et al., 2019). This could be said to more broadly reflect the dominant scientism present in the social sciences that it is argued has often neglected the humanistic concerns associated with social scientific research, in favour of a reductionist, idealized positivistic view (Cohen et al., 2007). Furthermore, caution has been made about the limitations of such a methodology which it is argued is fundamentally inappropriate as a mode of enquiry when applied to the social world of human beings, as it fails to recognize the moral and other qualities of humankind which are significant parts of the whole which should not be separated (Habermas, 1972, 1974; Horkheimer, 1972; Dornyei & Ryan, 2015; Dewaele et al., 2019).

Most of the research into SLA and language teaching is mainly quantitative in nature (Dufva, 2013). This research is often focused on SLA concerned with measuring the development of a learner's L2 knowledge (Hughes, 2002; Hughes & Szczepek-Reed, 2017). Language knowledge, however, is divided into two sub-categories: declarative knowledge such as vocabulary and grammar, and the ability to apply this knowledge correctly via utterances which are procedural knowledge (Jackendoff, 2002). With respect to research into speaking, there is still not a large amount, though it is growing (Hughes & Szczepek-Reed, 2017). There are complex and paradoxical reasons for this, which relate to the cognitive turn of the 1950s created by formal linguistics and its relationship with language education, some of which have been outlined in the previous section (Hughes & Szczepek-Reed, 2017, 22). While the historical climate changed and then the emergence of interest in sociocultural approaches to language eventually influenced language teaching, leading figures in theoretical linguistics had a low opinion of it as the source of empirical study, preferring idealized, non-contextualized sentences as the object of analysis, instead of speech corpora. This is an issue that is still a source of division between the formal linguistic school and the social-cognitive-functional schools to this day (Hughes & Szczepek-Reed, 2017).

Even more neglected is qualitative research into the experience of speaking in the EFL literature (Dufva, 2013). Given the relative abundance of formal SLA research into language teaching (Whong, 2011) and the aims of my research question which seeks to discover learner experiences, this book will examine these dimensions, in relation to the nature of adult EFL speaking. Moreover, given the focus on speaking as communication and more particularly as dialogue, specific interest is paid to these areas.

Much of the contemporary studies begin with the positive influence of dialogic teaching on the development of learners' speaking skills, as it has been shown to be dependent on the level of English and the level of motivation to learn the language (Elhassan & Adam, 2017). This contrasts with the more widespread and traditional Initiation–feedback–response (I.R.F.) communication in many Western nations, which is argued to limit the development of discourse and therefore thought (Alexander, 2006, 2020). Classroom dialogue, on the other hand, affords engagement, advances modes of thinking, increases understanding of topics, alongside improving longer-term educational skills and abilities. Three main caveats however have been identified regarding the efficacy of dialogic teaching, two of which draw attention to the significant role of the teacher: the first is needing to be high in language proficiency, and the second is aware of the dialogic teaching technique. It is also claimed that teaching the scientific method of supporting arguments is something that the teacher may have the responsibility to teach and enforce in order to develop debating and argumentation skills (El-Hassansan & Adam, 2017).

As Hunter (2012) notes, the emphasis in dialogic teaching on simultaneously developing fluency, accuracy and complexity in speaking, unhindered by teacher correction, increases speaking ability and learner confidence. Hunter also notes that correcting dialogic speaking is reported as being more effective when provided post-task in the form of written communication. At the level of monitoring and correction, dialogic speaking provides a balance between stimulating interlanguage growth via spoken communication and teacher pedagogical intervention via feedback. The effect of using CLT is also found to provide a solution to the skill acquisition of speaking posed by more traditional Grammar-Translation approaches which place little to no emphasis on speaking

(AL-Garni & Al-Muhammadi, 2019). In contrast, CLT is seen as offering a solution to these limitations. Such research highlights the importance of a teacher-led diagnosis of the specific context with regard to student skills, needs and the relevance the of curriculum topic. This suggests that cultural-social-affective dimensions of learner experience are fundamental in designing and planning curricula among adult EFL learners at university.

Additionally, dialogic teaching has been found to be superior to previous traditional Grammar-Translation methods which have been found to be inadequate for developing EFL speaking. Indeed, previous traditional Grammar-Translation methods have been found to be inadequate for developing spoken communication in some adult university contexts where a communicative-led approach to teaching speaking has been successful (Al-Garni & Almuhammadi, 2019). Teaching methods and materials that do not focus on preparing learners for real-world communicative situations beyond the classroom are reported by learners as being ineffective. This issue relates to the relative authenticity of curriculum materials or texts and has long been argued to be a common issue in some ELT contexts, however, it is dependent on the language level of the students and their goals as language learners (Nunan, 2004; Al-Garni & Almuhammadi, 2019, 5). Students' attitudes reveal the value of the topic – whether functional or abstract – as fundamental in motivating communication, and consequently driving acquisition and positive experience of the pedagogy. This suggests that the topics – as an aspect of the educational dimension – play a central role in promoting effective speaking.

Such calls for a similar reformation of speaking in adult ELT have been voiced (Kumaravadivelu, 1994) as a recommended principle for teaching as they 'maximize learning opportunity, facilitate negotiated interaction, minimize perceptual mismatches, activate intuitive heuristics, foster language awareness, contextualize linguistic input, integrate language skills, promote learner autonomy, raise cultural consciousness and ensure social relevance' (Kumaravadivelu, 1994; Celce Murcia & Brinton, 2014, 10–11). These principles are characterized as belonging to the third and most recent phase of post-methods, which began as a subset of practices within the CLT period in the early 1990s (Larsen-Freeman & Anderson, 2011) and yet also reflect key aspects of the first phase of communicative speaking approaches such as Curran's counselling-learning (1972) and community language learning (1976) from the early 1970s.

Dialogic speaking also possesses social-affective affordances. A Group Dynamics-Oriented Instruction as a form of CLT highlighted the relationship between the communicative and social-affective aspects of EFL classroom approaches. In Alikhani and Baheridoust (2017), communicative tasks and activities were also found to influence learners' willingness to participate due to increased motivation by resolving some of the issues which occur in communicative tasks, regarding conflict between learners. By placing greater importance on the learner experience in terms of motivation and developing 'conceptual and psychological predispositions' (Alikhani & Baheridoust, 2017, 44), the approach highlights the affordances of a holistic approach, providing a much broader and complete picture of the relationship between language attainment and experience. Such studies however are still representative of the other studies discussed so far that place an emphasis on trying to determine a correlation between the affective pedagogical shift (usually in the form of a communicative pedagogy) against the acquisition of grammar and vocabulary. In this manner, the definition of language learning could be seen as limited, in so far as the term 'holistic' when applied to education goes beyond a simple one-to-one correlation between affect and academic achievement. Rather, by introducing the affective dimension, there is a potential to make connections with all aspects of the language learning experience that may reveal previously neglected insights of great value (Curran, 1972; Arnold, 2011; Dufva, 2013).

The employment of the instruction of an explicit affective strategy for EFL university students as a way of improving speaking is positively evaluated by students when the employment of the affective strategies and speaking performance of learners are present (El-Sakka, 2019). This pedagogy is designed to address the commonly identified detrimental impact of low self-confidence identified in classroom language learning (Curran, 1972). The employment of psychological preparation for learning was based on humanistic criteria which were shown to break down communicative impasses in the EFL classroom. Whereas aspects of the affective dimension have been identified as causes of EFL teachers' barriers to teaching speaking, the findings suggest that fear of making mistakes, lack of self-confidence and lack of motivation were major obstacles for language students (Tawalbeh & Al-Asmari, 2015). It is argued that until such issues be addressed by teachers, and the educational institution at large, improvement of speaking skills will not be attainable.

Using debating as a communicative method where dialogue is emphasized is proposed as a solution to the plateauing effect, which signals a period in which a second language learner ceases to progress in the learning of a new language (Aclan & Aziz, 2015). One possible reason for this affordance is that when the curriculum content is not engaging, this can result in reduced motivation, which leads to plateauing (Richards, 2010). Debates create a context in which the necessity of vocabulary learning occurs which can be even more effective when pre-reading is prescribed by the teacher, giving the learners time to prepare and familiarize themselves with key vocabulary (Aclan & Aziz, 2015). Indeed, Aclan and Aziz report that students found it challenging to debate without the prior knowledge of vocabulary necessary to partake in the debate, without doing prior research which simultaneously involved learning new vocabulary associated with the unfamiliar topic. A task-orientated structure of the debates creates a staged process where language is learned and then used in a meaningful manner that engages learners during the debates. Learners' speech is also more effective due to the staging of the task, providing them with the time to prepare the language which they then include when debating. This can also be done by noticing new words when they are spoken during the debate, writing down the new words during the research phase, using dictionaries and translating the new vocabulary; finally, after this new input has been learned, using the words in context through interaction (Aclan & Aziz, 2015).

Overall, the evolution of teaching speaking according to Kumaravadivelu and Celce Murcia (2014) draws on aspects of the approaches and methods found in the last two historical phases, which emphasized speaking due to its increased efficacy of driving acquisition and the affective quality of learner experience. The recent research into speaking highlights the introduction of dialogical speaking as offering an alternative to a more traditional Grammar-Translation Approach, the former being strongly preferred by learners. This alternative, however, is not new, as Curran (1972) and Freire (1972, 1974) both demonstrated and argued for it at the beginning of the CLT era.

According to teaching assessment guidelines such as the CELTA (Cambridge English, 2021), the basic onus of putting into practice more up-to-date evidence-based practice is on the teacher. The degree to which such assessment is ongoing throughout a teacher's career, or the degree to which an individual teacher chooses to develop or upskill, is another question, however. From either perspective, it is evident that there are indeed some challenges to be overcome to improve the speaking ability of EFL students in this context. Once again, both Freire (1972) and Curran (1972) place a clear responsibility on teachers to be sufficiently informed and skilled, so as to ensure that their pedagogy offers both an effective promotion of SLA from the cognitive and broader educational perspective, while also emphasizing the role of affect and the social, that are not mutually exclusive.

5

Debating, Dialogic Teaching and Affect in Teaching and Learning English

Debating as teaching speaking in EFL

What has been highlighted so far is the importance of speaking as dialogue (Aclan & Aziz, 2015), as a way of improving cognitive goals such as vocabulary, communicative goals such as increased conversation and discussion (Alikhani & Bagheridoust, 2017), social goals such as increased engagement (Al-Ghamdi, 2017), educational goals such as improved relevance of content and critical thinking (Elhassan & Adam, 2017), and the humanistic goal of improved experience of EFL classes (Akerman & Neale, 2011).

As has been seen evidenced, one clear activity or task available to teachers for combining such affordances is through debating (Aclan & Aziz, 2015). This form of speaking has long been held in high esteem since ancient times throughout a number of diverse regions and has been found more recently – both outside of formal education and inside formal education, to be a powerful educational activity (Akerman & Neale, 2011). Debating requires the student to consider a topic or an issue, gain a thorough knowledge of it, and then express their position in a logical, clear, and coherent manner (Freely & Steinberg, 2014). The practice is also usually based on a topic of interest arbitrated by a panel or chair (Snider & Schnurer, 2006). Where it is most often found employed as an extracurricular competitive activity (Akerman & Neale, 2011), it is also employed as a form of pedagogy.

While a good deal of studies into the efficacy of debating in native-speaking studies have been done, only a small number of studies have demonstrated how debates have been used in foreign language education to great effect, though much more research is needed (Akerman & Neale, 2011).

Some of the benefits range from 'student perception data indicates that engaging in debate activities increases engagement' (Akerman & Neale,

2011, 18), and debates have been shown to improve the communicative skills of participants (Colbert, 1995; Akerman & Neale, 2011, 20). Additionally, debating as a communicative task has also been found to be meaningful, and authentic, as it engages learners' experiences and points of view. This is in comparison with more traditional grammar-translation models, which are focused on the texts provided by the teacher (Aclan & Aziz, 2015). It is also argued that in a continually globalized world reform of communication practices in EFL and language teaching still requires moving from a traditional teacher-centred model to a dialogue-based approach and that debating is one such method suited to this (Inoue & Nakano, 2004; Akerman & Neale, 2011, 16). Social and affective benefits such as increased confidence, self-esteem and broadening horizons – though not in relation to any language teaching research specifically – have also been demonstrated as affordances of debating in EFL (Akerman & Neale, 2011).

Interestingly, it is in the work of humanistic scholars, who appeared during the advent of the communicative period such as Freire that debate was first conceived as a fundamental language teaching method (Freire, 1972; 1974). In terms of the actual application of debating as a task spread across a series of lessons, or more simply as a one-off communicative activity, it is difficult to ascertain to what extent debating is employed as an activity in EFL or ESOL. Two of the major handbooks on English language teaching namely Harmer (2013) and Scrivener (2005) do recommend speaking discussion activities but do not use the term 'debate'. One weakness here is that such activities might not be exploited for their significant potential to make connections in developing other skills. The skill of reading, for example, could be incorporated into the pre-debate research stage as evidenced in my research and elsewhere (Akerman & Neale, 2011). Indeed, as discussed, debating is a form of speaking that is mainly argued for in Eastern foreign language contexts, and within those contexts, it is claimed to be a new and innovative method of teaching speaking (Aclan & Aziz, 2015).

That such comprehensive research into debating in TEFL is lacking has been perhaps indexical to the many questions and debates about the nature of language acquisition on a holistic level. What these dimensions that have been neglected could indicate is that Scientism continues to lead the way in studies into second language acquisition and language teaching research (Dufva, 2013). A combination of research into both the cognitive and the affective which enquires into learners' experience of learning could provide a holistic perspective, thus informing teacher practice and improving learner outcomes. This research method is also the one employed by Curran (1972) and Freire (1974) and on which they formulated their humanistic-orientated theories of education.

Dialogue and affect

The theoretical perspective assumed in this book rest on the foundations that have been placed on the relationship between these two pillars of language education, and that are still key to providing a deeper understanding between them. Curran's CLL (1976) which was concerned with dialogic speaking, and its earlier more general approach counselling-learning (1972), also emphasized the humanistic dimension of language learning. Though not traditionally included in this list of methods, but by now acknowledged as significant (Larsen-Freeman, 2011), Freire's seminal *Pedagogy of the Oppressed* originally published in 1970, and *Education for Critical Consciousness* originally published in 1974, also made strong proposals about the importance of dialogue in language learning and teaching. Additionally, Freire argued that fostering dialogue created a humanistic pedagogy. Indeed, the more explicitly humanistic discussions in the recent literature on the challenges of teaching speaking in EFL cite these developments in the 1970s as the first acknowledgement of the significance of this dimension (Larsen-Freeman & Anderson, 2011). The impact – at the time – of these scholars even spurred on the likes of heavyweight intellectuals such as Chomsky to comment and support these calls that were raised, during a time in US history, when due to a variety of social-political factors, the relationship between education and democracy was put into question (Chomsky, 2002).

The first wave of humanistic approaches to language teaching

What the aforementioned efforts regarding the nature of dialogic speaking in EFL highlighted is that the importance of the affective dimension in relation to teaching speaking in EFL can play a role in informing multiple factors that have been identified. This includes the cognitive (Aclan & Aziz, 2015), educational, communicative (Elhassan & Adam, 2017), social (Al-Ghamdi, 2017), and affective dimensions of pedagogical and curriculum planning, regarding speaking and EFL (Akerman & Neale, 2011).

In the beginning, when humanistic concerns in language teaching emerged during the 1970s, several approaches and methods that were based on the humanistic dimension of language learning, and were informed by what was then termed 'humanistic psychology', which had emerged in the previous decade, took shape in ELT (Larsen-Freeman & Anderson, 2011). These main methods were CLL, suggestopedia, the silent way, total physical response and critical pedagogy. A brief survey of their methods and rationale will be outlined, and the most pertinent approaches considered in more detail.

Despite their differences in approach and method, there were nonetheless some general humanistic concerns that they shared: All of these methods can be seen as following the previously discussed comprehension approach, which was based on conclusions about language acquisition derived from linguistics (Larsen-Freeman & Anderson, 2011). However, the main tenet of these methods was that the humanistic dimension of language learning was fundamental for acquisition. Suggestapedia was motivated by the belief that fear and lack of confidence inhibited the ability to learn a second language effectively. In this method, students are reassured and constantly supported by being given simple easy-to-learn instructions and guidance, often with the students – first language being utilized to scaffold learning. Visual materials and regalia are also used to convey meaning (Larsen-Freeman, 2011). The silent way proposed that learning processes are self-initiated and that their teaching must tap into and serve to trigger these inner cognitive resources. While the method is teacher-led the teacher rarely speaks, and instead uses gestures and a set of media such as cuisennaire rods to express sentence structures (Stevick, 1990). There are also feedback sessions where learners are encouraged to express their feelings about the learning process. Finally, the total physical response focuses on comprehension and input as the driving force of language acquisition. While being teacher-centred in terms of communication, it is believed that this reduces anxiety in the learner, who is never 'put on the spot' or forced to speak (Larsen Freeman & Anderson, 2011). The aforementioned methods arguably focus on developing the initial stages of foreign or second language development, though pay less attention to how the language can be developed beyond these stages.

In contrast, the two main approaches of this period that most clearly draw on the kind of communicative speaking that mirrors debating most closely were introduced by Curran (1972) and Freire (1972, 1974). These approaches and their methods offer a learning model that has as their goal the continued development not only of vocabulary, grammar and pronunciation as representing speaking skills but the practice of developing critical thinking through discussion. For debating to take place however in the L2 both of the methods proposed by Curran and Freire are designed to gradually build up the learner's knowledge.

Each method shared several of the humanistic pedagogical practices included in the prior methods described so far. Curran proposed counselling-learning, a general approach, and later CLL, as a more specific method (1972). He argued that due to the affective challenges associated particularly with speaking in a foreign or second language, such as anxiety, and other concerns about accuracy the affective dimension was fundamental for successful learning and teaching, i.e. for learners to be successful in learning to speak, they would need positive affective support from the teaching and the learning environment (Curran, 1972). His methods recommended the use of the L1 up until the learners felt comfortable with their L2 attainment, at which point he argued they would begin to speak in the L2.

At the same time, Paolo Freire argued for a similar approach to language teaching in which the potential positive affective value associated with speaking via dialogue was emphasized, thus providing a platform for individual and collective group expression, and honouring the voices of the foreign language learner who was at that time also part of a subjugated social group (Freire, 1972, 1974). The beginning of his pedagogy however was focused on identifying through interviews in the L1, a knowledge of the keywords and expressions concerned with the experience of the group, with a particular emphasis on language that expressed 'existential meaning (and thus the greatest emotional concern)' (Freire, 1974). This is followed by a second stage in which the phonemes of the language are taught via their contextualization with topics that emerge in the initial diagnostic stage; the idea being too closely associated with the formal aspects of the language, particularly the sound of the language with personal meaning. In the case of both Curran and Freire, they identified language pedagogy as special for what were ultimately similar reasons; they saw its potential to empower the individual through becoming an actor as opposed to a passive subject.

Curran's (1972) and Freire's (1972, 1974) most specific contributions to language teaching could, therefore, be argued as belonging to their end goals of prioritizing speaking through dialogue, to afford authentic expression. This is deemed to promote the positive-affective experience of expressing one's ideas and experiences which harmonize with content/curriculum; pedagogical processes and curriculum planning that were absent during the first three historical periods of teaching speaking that reduced this important skill to rote learning or role play (Howatt & Smith, 2014). Additionally, these considerations however do not stand alone but rather are integrated into a model that considers the cognitive, social, educational, communicative and affective dimensions; thus, representing human education as acknowledging the human as a unified being, and representing what Curran termed 'a whole-person model for education' (Curran, 1972).

Clearly, the approaches and methods associated with the first three periods of teaching speaking did not explicitly factor into these concerns. Instead, a focus on the purely cognitive aspects, which Curran (1972) refers to as the view of the human mind as mechanical, was the basis for pedagogical and curriculum planning. While progress has been made in the teaching of speaking in EFL (Howatt & Smith, 2014) ongoing reforms appear to be necessary to integrate these insights based on the arguments made during the 1970s by humanistic approaches to language teaching – and more recent work – in favour of a more holistic approach that comprises the affective dimension (Arnold, 2011; Dufva, 2013; Dewaele et al., 2019).

Later perspectives and developments in humanism and education

As this period gave way to the dawn of CLT, issues of humanism became controversial among some scholars and were challenged (Stevick, 1990). For example, it was argued that the permitting of students' non-participation, if they did not feel comfortable speaking in the L2, was in fact, inconsistent with the overall approaches. Additionally, post-modernist critiques were levelled at methods such as Curran's that were informed by psychotherapy, in so far as they were deemed to potentially 'subvert freedom' by prescribing what equated to 'good behaviour' (Stevick, 1990, 69). In defence of these humanistic approaches, Stevick points out, however, that these approaches and methods emphasized freedom and diversity. More recently, some have challenged the impact of humanistic approaches and suggested that they belong to an American-centric history of English language teaching, and are of less historical relevance in Europe (Howatt & Smith, 2014). Such exchanges may serve to highlight the cultural, political and philosophical nature of pedagogy at times, whether based on faith or philosophy. However, the line of humanistic scholars, while acknowledging differences among peoples, emphasizes equality and the similarities between humans (Curran, 1972; Freire, 1972, 1974).

Since Stevick's in-depth examination and clarification of the various goals of humanism in language teaching (1990), little explicit importance has been directed towards affect in relationship to ELT and teaching speaking research (Yan & Horwitz, 2008; Wu, 2010; Dufva, 2013). However, more broadly, there is evidence of an appreciation of its importance across the range of language skills. In one of the main entry-level language teacher training courses, its assessment criteria for the Certificate in English Teaching to Adults (CELTA) offer consideration of humanistic factors (Cambridge English, 2021, Table 1). As has already been introduced, the broader syllabus features five main topics ranging from learners and teachers, the teaching and learning context, language analysis and awareness, language skills: reading, listening, speaking, and writing, planning, and, resources for different teaching contexts, and developing teaching skills and professionalism. Within each of these criteria, there is a more detailed list of definitions of how these skills and competencies are defined for example in Cambridge English (2021). Some of these are explicitly affective, when, for example, considerations such as 'cultural, linguistic and educational backgrounds' or 'motivations for learning English as an adult' are stated, while others such as demonstrating the ability to employ 'key strategies and approaches for developing learners' language knowledge' evidence one of the many ways in which a language teacher meets the more cognitively orientated objective of developing language skills (Cambridge English, 2021, 5). The CELTA course is, however, short, consisting of a minimum of 120 hours of contact time. As such, the extent to which these criteria are replenished in the mind of the qualified TEFL teacher or guide them is another question. Indeed, a major concern is that there is an apparent and significant gap between TEFL research and practice (Howatt & Smith, 2014).

Though not specific to the skill of speaking, the history of affect in psychology as a part of SLA has expanded in some areas much more fully and considerably than others. In order for SLA to inform the instructive dimension in language learning an increasingly broader and more inclusive approach is argued by these researchers to necessarily involve the subjective aspects to a greater degree (Dewaele et al., 2019). Of greatest relevance to the concerns is the simultaneous development and integration of the subjective dimension in CHT which now comprises one of the two pillars of this book which I have so far termed 'affect' and 'humanism'. In very recent years the term 'positive psychology' (PP) has been adapted and asserted its role in applied linguistics, SLA and language teaching. However, approximately twenty years ago, around the time of the year 2000, an increase in actual research moving beyond theory and a small array of what had come to be considered less significant humanistic methods from the 1970s emerged (Howatt & Smith, 2014).

One may wonder if the current situation regarding what is now termed 'PP' and language teaching has taken for granted to some degree the affective dimension or perhaps it has become absorbed as an obvious or implicit factor in methods and approaches. This being said the research highlighted so far suggests that if so. such a disregard be reconsidered. Beyond language teaching however, there are broader calls such as those demonstrated by the current World Economic Forum (WEF) and the Organization for Economic Co-operation and Development Policy (OECD) (OECD, 2021; WEF, 2021). These organizations refer to affective awareness or humanism as relating to emotional intelligence (EQ) (WEF, 2021) or social and emotional skills (SES) (OECD, 2021), and cite research that argues that its role is fundamental in developing successful outcomes in education and work (Bradberry & Greaves, 2009; OECD, 2021). Furthermore, EQ has been identified as a fundamental skill that is vital for adult education (16–60 years of age) and development worldwide (OECD, 2021), alongside other more traditional conceptions of intelligence as demonstrated through skills such as literacy (OECD, 2013). More specifically, the research has resulted in an identification of five emotional skills – termed 'The Big Five' which have been implicated as being particularly significant for developing 'critical life outcomes' (OECD, 2015, 6). While the applicability of the research, however, has not yet been extended to the age group of the debate group participants who are over sixty, such a framework would be desirable and useful in increasing understanding of the role of SES in speaking in adult EFL.

Such contemporary research findings should not be surprising, given the original statements made about the relationship between earlier formulations of 'The Big Five', as highlighted in Curran (1972) and Freire (1974) regarding second language teaching and learning. As welcome as such formulations are, these key principles, appear – nonetheless – to be re-formulations of earlier work, perhaps due to the continued lack of implementation of such knowledge in the interim decades (Arnold, 2011; Dufva, 2013).

It is therefore, perhaps, not surprising that as the research considered shows, there is a belief and a desire among adult EFL learners that a CLT approach, informed by further insights from the post-methods era, is the most effective one for developing the important skill of speaking. This is in opposition to the apparently standard traditional grammar-translation approach which though still commonplace in many contexts is ineffective in achieving the desired goals for successful SLA (Whong, 2011; Howatt & Smith, 2014). Furthermore, the definition of efficacy provided by learners consists of a holistic approach to language study which includes the practice of the skill of speaking through a dialogic method such as debating. Based on the research reviewed so far however, the consideration of the affective dimension in TEFL is currently considered to be novel and innovative, at least as far as its actual application is concerned. Dewaele et al (2019) suggest that MacIntyre and Gregersen's PP (2012) reflects the renewal point of these efforts to mark out what was formerly referred to as either humanism or affect which was later followed in 2016 as a new starting point in which the beginnings of an acknowledgement of applied linguistics and a 'growing popularity of PP, and an exponential increase in publications in more mainstream journals' occurred.

Further developments regarding the role of affect in learning and language teaching

From the perspective of negative affective experience, there is an ever-increasing body of evidence that also demonstrates the detrimental role of negative stress on the cognitive development of young children (National Scientific Council on the Developing Child [2005/2014]) and negative stress on speaking performance in second languages in adults (Khan, 2010). In addition, the aforementioned major international research projects that have been undertaken by the OECD also argue for the consideration of affect and the social dimensions of education (OECD, 2021). Such studies therefore complement the claims of the first wave of the humanist movement which asserted that anxiety prevents language acquisition (Curran, 1972; Gattegno, 2010; Lozanov, 1978; Moskowitz, 1978; Krashen & Terrell, 2000).

In language teaching research, affect has been defined as 'related to aspects of emotion, feeling, mood or attitude which condition behavior' (Brown, 1999), and specifically in language teaching as a contextual concern with 'what goes on inside and between the people in the classroom' (Stevick, 1980; Arnold, 2011, 4). Arnold's elaboration of this position provides a more useful clarification of what this may mean in terms of criteria for teaching.

> The inside and between is basically what affect is about: on the one hand, the individual or personality factors (self-concept/self-esteem, anxiety, inhibition, attitudes, motivation, learner styles …) which we can consider as inside the learner, and on the other, the relational aspects which develop between the participants in the classroom – between students or between teacher and students – or possibly between learners and the target language and culture.
>
> (Arnold, 2011, 1)

Arnold, therefore, argues that the relationship between the inside and the between are fundamental consideration in language education, as it is as necessary as socially driven as it is personal; the metaphor of the inside and between reflects this. Language learning is different from other educational subjects, as 'language, after all, belongs to a person's whole social being; it is part of one's identity' (Williams, 1994; Arnold, 2011, 77). This is an additional reason for taking into consideration the affective dimension of language education, as there is a greater potential for the influence of negative affect to hinder learning. It can be seen as an additional reason for conflating the term used by Curran (1972) of including the affective dimension to achieve a 'whole-person' approach to language education, as all aspects of the person are impacted by affect.

Arnold's definition of affect as being divided between 'the inside and the between' as quoted earlier also reflects Vygotsky's conception of cognition. While the inside for Vygotsky is the 'inner plane' or the mind, and the 'between' is the 'external plane' which from an educational perspective is the classroom, and from the wider perspective – society (Vygotsky, 1978). Such concerns as argued for within humanistic language teaching, therefore, necessarily highlight the relationship between the social and affective dimension as not entirely mutually exclusive within the language learning context. This has been confirmed by the creation of the term 'social and emotional learning' (SEL) as referred to earlier, based on a great deal of empirical studies, including on adults (OECD, 2015). Combined, cognitive stimulation and growth for the language learner from the social plane with respect to learning grammar, vocabulary and pragmatics interact with the 'inside' subjective emotions that in language teaching is termed 'affect'. While this may seem a common-sense notion, by now it is a well-established and widely accepted learning theory that negative-affect arrests cognitive development (National Scientific Council on the Developing Child [2005/2014]), and performance, and that conversely, positive affect creates the conditions for cognitive development (Khan, 2010).

The issue of diversity and differentiation could also be faced in a more productive way when considered from the affective perspective (Arnold, 2011). If each learner can be communicated with greater sensitivity and understanding, then by showing this understanding, the learner can feel more positive about themselves and their relationship with their teacher, thanks to this rapport of acceptance of difference (Curran, 1972; OECD, 2015, 2021). In this sense, instead of viewing diversity as problematic and countering it with conflict and discipline, it may be that bridges could be built that increase mutual understanding between teacher and student and between students. This then enables the teacher to teach and the learner to learn, as positive affect is increased. This reflects a student-centred approach to teaching, whereby, the teacher does not close themselves off from the students by only lecturing them, but rather reaches out to form a particular relationship based on a mutual understanding with each student (1972). This was conceptualized by Curran (1972) during the first wave of humanism in his counselling-learning whole-person approach to language teaching, as reflecting the relationship of the counsellor with the patient, though both are taken to possess each role interchangeably depending on the type of communication taking place at any given point during a lesson; the teacher themselves being in need of acceptance and harmony with the learners. Such an approach requires a dynamic and holistic understanding of the multiple dimensions of the educational process, though perhaps requires a sacrifice on the part of some teachers depending on their character (Freire, 1972). A responsibility is also placed on the teacher to think beyond a narrow conception of delivering academic content as their main aim, and instead, considering that intellect can be defined as much as a cognitive capacity as it is an emotional one (OECD, 2021). In so doing, the teacher may extend their role to developing affective strategies to more fully engage learners by getting to know them more; an aspect also of the social dimension.

Such proposals that were made at the beginning of the humanistic era during the 1970s reflect later perspectives on humanism and language teaching whereby 'the quantum shift we search for in our ability to facilitate more effective learning (as teachers) lies in a shift at the level of our attitudes, our awareness and our attention to process' (Underhill, 1989, 260). In this sense, the innovation is not technological but rather human, the process being the conscious way in which a lesson is organized and orchestrated. Indeed, the term 'process syllabi' is a synonym for the analytic syllabi proposed by Thornbury and Meddings (2010) which is based on a personalized curriculum where the learner is considered the source of content. Such a curriculum supports what has been identified as a link between inner confidence and inner and outer competence in the second language (Rubio, 2007; Andrés, 2009). In light of this, freer speaking as afforded by debating as a communicative method of teaching speaking possesses such potential properties given that 'experiencing real achievement in using the target language in meaningful communication is the surest route to self-esteem' (Arnold, 2011, 6).

In conclusion, though we are living in the post-methods period that can be seen as an extension of the CLT period and has been doing so since the 1970s, there has still been an ongoing process of this realization, where much research is needed (Dufva, 2013). But once again, the reason for prioritizing speaking is twofold: by working on increasing self-esteem, learner motivation can be created (Curran, 1972; Freire, 1974; Arnold, 2011). In this way, motivation is not only the motivation to begin the study of a language realized by the student but to discover that motivation via the teacher attending to the affective dimension of their pedagogy. This positive fostering of the 'L2 Self' has been argued to be a potentially powerful base from which to improve learner achievement (Dornyei & Ushioda, 2021). These considerations are by no means limited only to the learner, however. The affective experience and development of the teacher are also central to these goals and should be the very foundation of their own personal development (Arnold, 2011). The trajectory of personal growth argued for in humanist language teaching (Gattegno, 2010; Curran, 1972; Stevick, 1990) has more recently argued that it should mirror also that of the development of the teacher as a cognitive-emotional being or simply as a 'person' (Arnold, 2011; Mercer, 2018). And it is, as was argued by both Curran and Freire long ago, that dialogic speaking has the greatest potential to realize such growth and improve learning outcomes.

Ultimately, it remains the case that the humanistic dimension has been identified as a key factor in language teaching, not only regarding a simple one-to-one correspondence between acquisition and anxiety, but regarding a broader set of considerations that correspond to the educational, cognitive and social, communicative dimensions, and the topic to which the next section and following chapters will seek to elucidate.

Contemporary research into affect and speaking

Evidence of the efficacy of debating as a form of dialogic speech that possesses the potential to provide a holistic, and humanistic approach to teaching speaking is found mainly in the East. It is significant that some of these insights are derived from learner attitudes and experiences about English language learning in formal contexts, primarily in universities.

The employment of functional dialogic speaking activities, teaching relaxation and mindfulness, and allowing the support of the first language and mime, have been found to increase acquisition and increase their positive evaluation of speaking in class (Prabhavathy & Mahalakshmi, 2012). Atmosphere, material, methods and techniques are all aspects of a humanistic teaching approach that can improve the experience of speaking in class. Though a broad number of factors have been suggested here, it appears that the bulk of studies defines the affective dimension in speaking as relating to concerns of speaking anxiety among learners. Research into anxiety and foreign language speaking is extensive in formal educational contexts (Arnaiz & Pérez-Luzardo, 2014; Baran-Łucarz, 2014; Pishghadam, 2016; Toubot et al., 2018; Setiawan, 2018; Liu & Xiangming, 2019; Meigouni & Shirkani, 2020). However, anxiety is only one aspect of the affective dimension as defined by its earliest adherents (Curran, 1972) and even more recently (Arnold, 2011). The most pressing question for an educator in relation to this topic might be what the cause of this anxiety is. In order to ameliorate or maximize learner experiences of speaking in EFL, the literature on EFL adult speaking demonstrates that the answer is a holistic one that corresponds to multiple aspects of the overall educational experience (Arnold, 2011). Furthermore, research that seeks to consult learners regarding their experiences more broadly can also inform more about the affective dimension, as research into speaking in EFL will demonstrate. As we have seen, the various aspects of the affective dimension, including speaking anxiety have been attributed to pedagogy and curriculum, two factors that are the responsibility of the teacher; as evidenced in teacher assessment: Cambridge English (2021). In this sense, it might be more pertinent to utilize such findings in teacher training and educational policy development instead of carrying out more research into 'anxiety' alone. Indeed, among the possible sources of foreign language speaking anxiety (FLSA) (based on Young's [1991] FLSA scale) that individual factors such as 'teacher personality, teaching style, teacher attitude, etc. – have an impact on FLSA' (Han et al., 2016, 8). In a Japanese university context, the teacher has also been attributed as the main source of learner anxiety (Effiong, 2015). In contrast, the employment of students' individual communication strategies could aid them in reducing anxiety (Meigouni & Shirkani, 2020). Meigouni and Shirkani recommend that learners be taught what were found to be effective communication strategies, specifically accuracy-orientated strategies where the learner focused on employing correct pronunciation, grammar and vocabulary. Interestingly, this approach would still place the onus on the teacher to teach learners how to reduce anxiety in speaking. Cheng-Chang Tsai (2018) also employed a pedagogical shift to reduce anxiety during speaking, which included the teaching of communicative strategies. Specifically, this comprises of management and planning, cognitive, communicative-experiential, interpersonal and affective speaking strategies. The pedagogical shift was found to lower anxiety in learners regardless of their level of proficiency.

Baran-Łucarz (2014) however found support for previous studies that showed a strong correlation between learner anxiety in speaking and lack of confidence in pronunciation. This could be correlated with Meigouni and Shirkani's (2020) findings about students' prioritization of accuracy as an anxiety reduction technique. In an Iranian university study, Pishgadam et al. (2016) found that in contrast to other skills, the emotions experienced in speaking by students were overwhelmingly positive. In another university context in Spain however, Arnaiz & Pérez-Luzardo (2014) also report speaking to be the skill that creates the most anxiety in EFL students.

Setiawan (2018) in a university setting found that self-confidence but not anxiety had the clearest influence on speech achievement. As such, she recommends that teachers provide opportunities in class for students to practice speaking in front of the class to increase their confidence (Tridinanti, 2018). This recommendation, however, may be better informed perhaps by further research as to whether this is a way in which this objective could be best ameliorated. Toubot et al. (2018) across three Libyan universities also found self-confidence to be the main determiner of anxiety level. As Meigouni and Shirkani (2020) highlight, communicative strategies – which could be taught – were found to lower student anxiety in speaking. In a similar manner, Anandari (2015) recommended that teachers provide reflective exercises to support students to overcome issues of anxiety with speaking, which were reportedly related to fear, shyness and feeling uncomfortable. By identifying the sources of their negative emotions but also identifying their strengths, she found that students' anxiety was lowered. Buriro and Siddique (2015) on the other hand, assign and attribute learners' anxiety to learner attitude. They highlight that students' insistence on trying to speak with a particular accent, unrealistic belief in the time necessary to reach the required language proficiency, and the perception of making mistakes as a more significant barrier all served to increase anxiety.

Wu (2010) examined the relationship between language learners' anxiety and learning strategy in the CLT classroom at a Chinese university. The authors discuss the attitudes experienced by learners of the CLT approach to speaking contrasted with the grammar-translation method in relation to the level of anxiety experienced. It was found, as in other studies that while the CLT approach is generally preferred for humanistic, communicative, educational, social and cognitive reasons, it was the affective dimension of CLT which also presented the greatest anxiety. As claimed in the studies highlighted above, while the CLT method is more attractive to learners, it was nonetheless found that some caution and consideration of local contextual issues are fundamental to maximizing its affordances. It was also found that teachers play the initial and most significant role in creating a foundation for CLT to take place effectively, by ensuring a positive educational environment that ensures that students feel comfortable. Yan & Horwitz (2008) carried out a qualitative set of interviews followed by a grounded theory analysis of learner experiences and attitudes on the role of anxiety in EFL among adults. This study represents a very rare example of such a study. Using an anxiety scale, a range of students who suffered varying levels of anxiety were selected and interviewed. The detailed interviews provide a comparatively rich description of learner attitudes and experience of the factors which create anxiety in EFL. Eleven themes from a previous focus group study were utilized to base the interview questions. The study actually produced eleven regional differences: language aptitude; gender; foreign language anxiety; language learning interest and motivation; class arrangements; teacher characteristics; language learning strategies; test types; parental influence; comparison with peers and achievement. Given its overwhelmingly significant role, the author's recommendation for further research is to consider both the personal and sociocultural factors associated with language learning, given its potential negative impact.

Though this book is primarily concerned with adult EFL and debating, it is worth noting that many of the same claims regarding the various holistic affordances of debating are supported in recent research into state school pedagogy of EFL. This is demonstrated in Cinganotto's research in three Italian middle and high schools where both teachers and students reported a wide range of benefits in improving both their experience of learning and their academic outcomes (2019). These include language skills such as listening and speaking that learners from elementary (A2) level and upwards can engage in and increase in proficiency, soft skills that possess humanistic affordances such as helping students to understand, respect others and foster teamwork and cooperation, in addition to being fun and increasing the students' passion for the subject. Debating was also found to increase subject knowledge, however, in particular as a way of reviewing and reinforcing rather than introducing new knowledge (Cinganotto, 2019).

Chapter summary and research questions

The contemporary research into dialogic speaking as a superior alternative to non-dialogic speaking – though rare – suggests that it nonetheless is favoured by learners based on their beliefs and experiences. Little research, however, is concerned with investigating the role of dialogic speaking or student experiences of speaking more generally. Therefore, there is a significant gap in the research to which my research aims to contribute. Contemporary research into the role of emotion found in the previously discussed, and the similar theories put forward mainly by Curran and Freire in relation to it, also highlights that a gap in awareness and implementation of these approaches persists, and further research is seemingly required in order to support these arguments, encourage dissemination and implementation.

Such assertions suggest that a holistic approach to teaching speaking in a strong communicative form that integrates the skill of dialogic speaking and the affective dimension into the other more traditionally accepted dimensions is absent, however. And that approaches and methods that take these factors into consideration in terms of pedagogy and curriculum planning could suitably be drawn on to remedy this apparent imbalance are also lacking. Furthermore, it is my proposal that particular attention be paid to the fact that a greater emphasis on speaking, of the dialogic variety – argued for since the beginning of the communicative period be considered as an approach that potentially can kindle the multidimensional aspects of the educational experience and produce a positive transforming affective experience for both learner and teacher alike.

Despite the attested findings that demonstrate that negative affective experience impedes cognitive development in children and performance in adults most research in the field persists in basing the relationship between language teaching and second language teaching research on the purely cognitive dimension of grammar-vocabulary acquisition. Although the absence of such research might also suggest that this reflects the current state of teaching practice in TEFL, few studies that evaluate this dimension of the educational experience are currently available to support this position. Nonetheless, contemporary scholars of humanism and language teaching state that the aims of creating a low anxiety atmosphere, confidence raising and a chance to succeed are important affective factors that instructed language learning should continually bear in mind.

The following research questions aim to discover the extent to which a debate pedagogy affords these aims:

- What are the experiences of adult EFL participants in a debate group?
- What can these experiences tell us about teaching speaking in adult EFL?

6

Debate Curriculum and Pedagogy

The debate group

In 2017, I was invited to chair a debate group that provided an ideal context in which to research using debates to teach EFL as a holistic pedagogical method. Though at the time of planning my main teaching context was a TEFL secondary school, the smaller scale of the adult debate group and access considerations made it more feasible to research. I should mention however, that my teaching in two secondary schools in Italy made frequent use of debate as a method of teaching speaking, and was certainly influential in my interest and decision to choose the research topic and question. Indeed, there is growing evidence in first language research of the numerous affordances of employing debate in secondary-level education (Kennedy, 2009). The school context in which I worked and carried out the research mostly provides English courses to children, teenagers and university students who wish or are required to sit Cambridge language exams for entry into schools that require a higher level of English, university courses that are taught in English, whether in Italy or in other countries. The vast majority of students are Italian, and many are native to the city or region. The city is considered to be relatively prosperous and based on the expense of the courses would suggest that the socio-economic background of learners is middle class. In this sense, the debate group fits into this socio-economic backdrop, in so far as the participants are all retired professionals. On the other hand, their age and motivation represent a distinct anomalous group, as they are all over sixty and attend the group as a leisure activity. The school is the only such context in which the participants can partake in such an activity and therefore provides a unique educational opportunity.

The research began within this same context which I had already been chairing since October 2017. Each week a topic was introduced couched in a debate question and a debate would ensue. Some participants would make notes and occasionally consult an English dictionary when necessary. From January 2019 until June 2019, two sets of interviews were undertaken. The first set comprised one-to-one individual interviews with each of the eight participants in January and February, followed by a focus group interview. The interviews explored the experiences of the participants and reflections on their prior and current learning experiences in the debate group. After the interviews, a pedagogical shift was applied based on participant feedback. This involved the introduction of an additional stage in which each participant had an uninterrupted period of five minutes at the beginning of the debate in which they could put forward their response to the debate question. Towards the end of the research period, a second group interview followed by a second run of final one-to-one interviews took place. Each debate lasted for seventy-five minutes, on a late Friday afternoon, over the period of seven and a half months, from October until the end of May of each school year.

Given the lack of research that seeks to understand student experience of dialogic speaking, and more particularly debating as a method of teaching EFL from a naturalistic perspective, the first question is: What are the experiences of adult EFL participants in a debate group? Contemporary research (Khan, 2010; Arnold, 2011; Liu & Jackson, 2011; Dufva, 2013; Baran-Łucarz, 2014; OECD, 2015) and theoretical approaches such as Curran (1969, 1972) and Freire (1972, 1974) highlight how the experiential dimension of education, comprising both pedagogy and curriculum provide important insights into the worth of a given teaching method. The second question: How could these experiences inform teaching speaking in adult EFL, therefore, aims to utilize the findings to provide a greater understanding of adult speaking in TEFL and debating in adult TEFL? The questions posed aim to provide a clear and practical framework for the practitioner, while also contributing to ongoing contemporary research.

Debate pedagogy and curriculum

The existing format and topics of the debate group were somewhat undefined when I first became chair in October 2017. However, as time went by, I sought to identify topics that possessed a better fit between the participants and their interests. By the time the research began, I had been able to refine the process of topic selection which was based on carefully listening and making notes during the debates, over a period of over a year. I would make notes about the topics and the participant's contributions with an increasing awareness of the dual practitioner concerns associated with curriculum planning, but also the role of the researcher. Topics ranged from 'the legacy of the Roman empire for Italians' to 'the nature and status of the EU', with each topic drawing on their experiences or knowledge. An extraordinarily rich contribution was consistently made based on the variety of the participant's life experiences. The structure consisted of proposing a debate question with some general background to the topic, at the beginning of each debate. The debate would then ensue, without any formal structure to the talk. It was, therefore, a two-staged process that required no preparation for the participants, and required no follow-up study. This format changed significantly, however, as a result of the interviews (see Table 2). Despite this more structured approach which has more in common with standard debate types (see Rybold & Harvey-Smith, 2013), it did not have much in common with the vast majority of methods, i.e. an intentionally competitive aspect. In this sense, it was more representative of debate as discussion, and indeed my observational notes throughout the period of the research recorded how the group had developed a natural process of stages through which they would progress.

Regarding the topics, though I had initially encouraged participants to propose debate topics themselves they were not forthcoming. As such, I continued to choose topics that I assumed the participants would have some familiarity with – and have opinions on – based on their interest in history,

Table 2 Pre- and post-interview debate structure

Debate structure pre-interviews	Debate structure post-first set of interviews
1) Debate question posed at beginning of debate	1) Debate topic posed at the end of debate.
	2) Participants research topic, prepare thesis
2) Free debate, no imposition on turn taking, pre-reading or post-reading	3) Debate question is provided at the start of the debate so as to remind participants
	4) Each participant is given up to five minutes to deliver their thesis
	5) Participants engage in freer debate, chaired by teacher-chair who occasionally supports the discussion or assists with language items
	6) At the end of the debate the new debate topic is provided, and the cycle goes on

current affairs and life experience. As time went by and I learned more about the interests and knowledge of the group as a whole, I would spend the week in between the debates considering and sometimes searching for possible topics. I aimed for a combination of historical and contemporary topics and issues, many of which would have relevance to the group. I made a habit of this prior to the period of research, and before, during and after. After the first set of interviews, a pedagogical shift was called for and put into place which altered the structure of the debates, but not the topics.

Chapter summary

The educational context of the debate group was important in shaping the evolution of the approach to the debates and led to further stimulation for pedagogical innovation (see Chapter 9). In this way, the debate group suggests that practitioner research in a style that shares much in common with action research can indeed inform and ameliorate educational practice, both regarding curriculum and pedagogy.

7

The Debate Curriculum and Pedagogy: What We Did

A debate group of four experiences

The data analysis produced four main themes: the debate group as a Communicative, Educational, Cognitive, and Social experience. The breadth of the themes suggests a holistic experience, as depicted by the four-pointed star which represents the four main themes converging on their experience of them (Figure 1). The unity and balance of the four themes are represented by the symmetry of the four-pointed star; the representation of affect at the core of the star reflects the experiential angle of the research – in that participants were interviewed about their experience of cognition, education, communication and the social. For example, the processing of vocabulary in listening or speaking is a cognitive act but is experienced as stressful in either a positive, negative or neutral manner depending on the individual. The educational experience may relate to the participant's experience of a debate topic on a similar evaluative scale; for example, they may have particularly enjoyed a given topic in which they learned something new or alternatively, a topic may have been discussed which offended them. The communicative experience could be experienced and evaluated according to the extent to which a participant feels that they had been given sufficient time to express their views on a topic. Finally, the social experience could be determined by whether or to what degree they felt their meeting with fellow participants was integral to their enjoyment of the debates or whether it was merely an instrumental necessity, i.e. to partake in a dialogic debate at least one debating partner is needed. From this perspective, the diagram could also be said to represent a process in which the four external themes which are illustrated as points of the star are the source of this separate concept of affect. In this way, these four themes activate affective experiences. Despite these categories, however, the model is situated within the broader

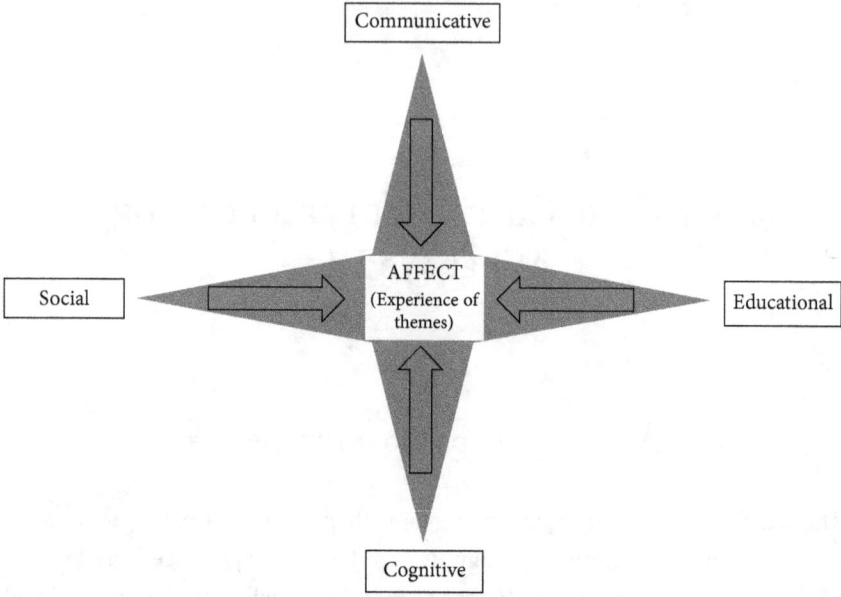

Figure 1 Four pointed star of educational experience.

perspective of prioritizing learner experience, through the debate pedagogy as a potentially humanistic form of education.

Although each theme will be described in the order in which they can be seen to emerge in the process of the activity of the debate, ultimately, however, all themes are interdependent, and thus reflect a holistic experience of the debate group and its affordances as humanistic education.

In line with the logic of the four-pointed star (Figure 1) through the coming together of the social and communicative, the cognitive and educational are stimulated, eventually resulting in an affective experience. Nonetheless, all the experiences of each theme are affective and therefore this theme is embedded in each of the themes presented.

A communicative experience

The theme of the debate as a communicative experience emphasized the various affordances of dialogue found in debating and its potential as a form of humanistic education. While there were some tensions brought about by such communication, the dialogic debate was experienced mostly as positive.

The following quote from Arturo's first interview conveys the connection between communication, education and affect that was expressed by many of the participants:

> Exchanging your opinions with others is important because you communicate with them and communicating is a way of enlarging your knowledge and offering your opinions to others and therefore this enriches your way of living. So debating is important because it is a way of exchanging; it is a way of getting and offering as well. (Arturo, first interview)

While Atena emphasized the positive experience of expressing:

> I could express myself because I was well. (Atena, final interview)

The debate group was more generally experienced debating as exchanging opinions by a number of participants:

> You don't come here to study language, you come here to have an exchange of opinion. (Valentina, first interview)

> There is a very good moment of exchanging our considerations and our mind. (Maria-Grazia, final interview)

Alessandra provided a clear rationale of how the communicative act of exchange can be seen not as a stand-alone activity or task, but rather one that involves the individual on a deeper, affective level:

> It's important to exchange ideas about situations and about your feelings and your sentiments and your way of life and how you can live or what can make you happy or not happy or about human values this is the most important and this is the most interesting for me ... the feelings that are in the human sphere, humanity, the chance to exchange our ideas and feelings about humanity in all senses. (Alessandra, final interview)

This form of exchange necessarily however was mainly viewed from a receptive communicative viewpoint. The chance to listen instead of expecting to speak was the most prized experience of the debate group. There were a variety of reasons given for this preference. In some cases, the motivation was based on affect and a consideration of the participant's perception of their ability:

> I try to express my opinion in the best way I can but sometimes I prefer just to listen to others, because sometimes they know a lot of things absolutely better than I do. (Maria-Grazia, First Interview)

Atena in her final interview said that she preferred listening and that the communicative dynamics encouraged one to become humble.

> Atena in her final interview said that she preferred listening and that the communicative dynamics encouraged one to become humble. (Atena, final interview)

Participants commented on the ease of communicative dynamics in the debate group, as a preference for listening was also seen to reduce the pressure on individuals to speak:

> The debate is comfortable because you can choose whether to listen or not. If you want to speak you can speak but if you don't you can just listen. If you are with a teacher and you follow the lesson it is difficult to abstain, so it's more stressful with one-to-one lessons. (Alessandra, first interview)

This same point was echoed in a similarly affective way by others:

> I'm not satisfied with my speaking, so I prefer listening because it's less important. I don't have to strive to listen, it's easy on my mind. (Valentina, first interview)

Participants commented that the communicative dynamics allowed them to be themselves, not feeling forced to play a particular communicative role:

> For me, it's more useful to listen. My debating skills are limited. In my opinion, in it is better to listen, when you have listened to all the opinions you can contribute and give your opinion, in every case not only in the debate group. When I talk with friends and family I prefer to first listen and then give my opinion. Because you give your opinion on what you have listened to ... based on what has been said. (Salvatore, first interview)

Value was given to the act of listening as training participants to be more respectful, tolerant and empathetic:

> In debating one gets an experience of being forced to understand and of not minding if what they are saying is interesting to you. But you must be patient and tolerant, so you must be humble in order to understand what they are saying. (Arturo, first interview)

Another rationale expressed was how communication could lead to personal growth, as a consequence of their courage and willingness to attend a group in which people were not assured – through already existing friendships – that their views would be shared by others. Participants noted that this aspect of the context is brought to the surface through the particular communicative act of debating:

> Debating is important because the more you become aware of others' views and build knowledge of the world the more you grow ... not only your opinion, your

knowledge but you enlarge your view. If you only debate with people that have the same opinion as you it's a good thing, but you can't enlarge your point of view or have intellectual growth. If you pretend to have the truth it's better to debate with people who have your opinion, but what's the truth? (Salvatore, first interview)

In a similar manner, Atena remarked that the debate group was about:

learning to respect your limits and accepting them. (Atena, first interview)

She also reported how she felt that the debate group helped her to reflect on how she could improve her sense of empathy:

by listening and being respectful and non-judgmental of others' views. (Atena, first interview)

Despite this aspect of the debate group as perhaps being about risk, Atena remarked that my role as the chair in managing communication when there could be a breakdown in communication or a lull provided:

a safety net for us. (Atena, final interview, field notes)

Disagreements were not experienced negatively, rather, they were seen as affording a positive change to take place in the individual:

I think the debate group is important for confrontation ('comparing'). (Maria-Grazia, first interview)

... I think you have to dialogue with an opponent because if you present an idea but your opponent presents a different one, but we try to find something together. Maybe it's important for growth ... growth, for both, I think. Of course, dialogue is sometimes not because it depends on the person (laughs). it's impossible sometimes (laughs). (Maria-Grazia, First interview).

Laura went one step further by attributing the role played by contrasting opinions with education: the initial cause being the act of communication, however:

Sometimes I find myself not agreeing with people but it's useful to not always agree because you can exchange in my opinion your opinion and exchange with other people and learn more about the topic. (Laura, first interview)

There is a simultaneous educational aspect to the way in which these participants described their experience here, as they explain that through such communication, learning necessarily occurs. As such, dialogue is expressed as possessing a transformational quality – both on an individual and broader societal level:

> Many times, you think that your opinion is the best but not always is it the best. And it's not always the only option. If you debate you can become aware that there are different opinions and points of view. (Salvatore, first interview)

Despite this positive consensus on the nature of the communication in the debate group, participants did nonetheless experience some difficulties. The Importance of turn-taking and each member having a chance to speak, prior to the pedagogical shift in which stricter time-sharing rules were implemented and enforced was repeatedly cited as the main negative experience of the debate group:

> The only problem is that ... unacceptable time sharing ... in our discussions. So, to allow everyone to speak and understand – because sometimes ... someone concentrates the time on himself and steals sometimes other's time, and therefore it is good to leave room for everyone, to explain your own point of view and to understand what everyone has been saying. It is necessary to speak and to be enabled to speak and to be enabled to understand. (Arturo, first interview)

At times, this was reported as resulting in a breakdown of comprehension and expression:

> It can be confusing; you know how two or three persons at the same time speak together. (Salvatore, first interview)

Partaking in such a community as a means of fulfilling positive affective experiences however was contrasted with some negative experiences. These aspects were associated with perceived weaknesses of the initial debate format that involved a higher degree of freer speaking, most particularly prior to the pedagogical shift, whereby participants felt that even turn-taking and talk time were not being permitted:

> I want to add something but many times I can't succeed. (Salvatore, first interview)

The challenge of using EFL despite it being one of the key aspects and motivations for partaking in the debates was also seen at times to contribute to a certain level of insecurity about one's ability:

> I feel like I'm being judged (by the other participants) for my English. (Alessandra, second interview)

> I'm a bit anxious but I go and I try ... I say sorry in advance but I try to go on. (Laura, second interview)

In each case, these experiences can be seen as representing barriers or obstacles to the desired outcome of the debate, which is to arrive at a positive experience of education, through dialogue, which according to the participants was regularly achieved. Clearly, this initial approach had a negative impact on the affective experience. When, however, halfway through the sampling period this was adjusted, the change was seen as improving the experience of the debate group:

> I think that it was a very good thing to give time for everyone to speak. (Osvaldo, final interview)

Similar sentiments were reported in the first group interview, as participants said the pedagogical shift of a three-minute time limit was viewed by most to be a good time limit for both speaker and listener. This also reduced stress while speaking and increased comprehension. It was also perceived by one participant as increasing discipline which was seen as important (first focus group).

The other main complaint, albeit reported by a small number of participants was the perceived diversity of language levels and communicative abilities. This was experienced as negative insofar as it apparently impeded the communicative flow:

> I think that's up to you to try to compensate for that considering that the matter is here … but the material is this, so it would be up to you to try to compensate for the others. (Osvaldo, final interview)

Osvaldo was referring to me as the teacher, here. He believed that my role as chair was to intervene, in cases where – he felt – other participants required language support. In this case, the debate group was perceived as an ELT context in which learners receive language instruction. Most of the participants did not speak about this, though others acknowledged that some form of language teaching was at least taking place.

Arturo provided a clear rationale as to why this issue can present a communicative barrier and impede comprehension:

> People who are the most interesting in debates are people who of course speak good quality English … you have difficulties in understanding … not so good people who don't use good English because you can't enter their minds … you can't really get what they want to say because they say it in a bad manner in English. (Arturo, first interview)

The issue of expression and comprehension can be seen from different perspectives. Alessandra explained how the act of thinking – itself – is a part of this challenge for participants. As she explained, a consideration of communicative style is also necessary in order to appreciate individual differences:

> Some people speak very quickly and have all their ideas just perfect, and another person is not so quick but their ideas are good in the same way. For example, student x sometimes speaks very fast, and I have difficulty following him and he always says very interesting things. Student Y on the other hand is slower but sometimes it seems that he has difficulties in speaking what he says is interesting too; so, they have different ways of expressing their views. (Alessandra, first interview)

The communicative dimension is expressed as essentially a binary division between speaking and listening. The communicative dynamics which take place, are at times complex, and are clearly described as mainly being positive; though at times there exist challenges. These perspectives often use evaluative language that often expresses the participant's feelings or experience about on the educational dimensions, and as such can be seen as providing feedback on the extent to which the method is humanistic.

An educational experience

The theme of debating as an educational experience emphasized the experience of the debate topics and the English language learning dimension. The experience of both aspects was enhanced by the role of peers as educators, as opposed to the chair/educator.

Maria-Grazia who was simultaneously attending a general conversation course asserted:

> In my conversation class, we never talk about so high issues, or intellectual issues. (Maria-Grazia, first interview)

While for the purposes of her conversation class – lighter topics were appropriate – she reported that the topics were highbrow and therefore initially made her question whether she would be able to cope with the course from both a language and an intellectual perspective. Her doubts were also founded on it being her first year of attending the debates:

> I thought that maybe it was not for me, that it was too high a level, but then I thought, maybe it could be important just to listen to the other peoples' opinions, and its always a chance to learn something more, because you are always talking about important things. (Maria-Grazia, First Interview)

Elsewhere it was asserted:

> Good technical items (should be) discussed, not only things that are not so important. (Arturo, first interview)

Though debating to some degree relies on subjective opinions and experiences, it was nonetheless made clear that there were some unwritten ground rules that should guide the calibre of the topics and how they are approached. Osvaldo contrasted his experience of the debate group with other forums that he was a member of:

> The most valuable thing ... that's not common (is to) have discussions at a good cultural level. Discussions (can) go down to everyday matters or demagoguery, or to unsubstantiated points of view, so the advantage for me is this. (Osvaldo, First interview)

In part, due to the intellectual nature of the topics, they were also experienced as being engaging. Again, this was contrasted with participants' other experiences, in this case of one-to-one lessons:

> In a private lesson, it is only for the language, so you are less motivated. And when we talk in a very free way the topic was very limited; life, your family, your work, once twice then it's very boring. The DEBATE GROUP engages you. (Salvatore, first interview)

Several participants commented on the educational experience of the debates, as this was seen as increasing learning about the topics:

> It is interesting to debate and to have dialogue. In my opinion you learn more in the debate because many times there are topics that interest you. The interest in a matter is fundamental. If you have limited interest in a matter, you learn a limited amount. (Arturo, first interview)

> I have learned about subjects that previously I could have much interest in and so this is an enrichment in my view. (Laura, second interview)

The engaging nature of the topics was reported by several participants as stimulating further learning about the topic at home:

> The topic of the conversation is usually quite stimulating ... every topic was quite interesting. (They are) subjects to be thought about, I can continue to think of the subject after six o'clock on a Wednesday. (Valentina, first interview)

> If I don't understand so well or if I don't know much about the topic, I am stimulated at home to satisfy my curiosity. (Laura, second interview)

Participants commented in the first group interview which took place after the pedagogical shift that setting the participants the task of researching the forthcoming topic a week in advance resulted in gaining a deeper knowledge of the topic because they could participate in the debate with knowledge from their research. The emphasis in the one-to-one interviews, however, was on learning about the topics through peer learning. When we talk about history, politics and social events, we acquire knowledge. For example, Osvaldo is quite educated and knowledgeable about history and science.

> I have learned many things from him and Arturo, and Alessandra and their experiences in other countries. (Salvatore, first interview)

Maria-Grazia also described how:

> You (the debate group) are always talking about important things ... I think it's very good, for example, Osvaldo is very good at History ... I read a lot too but not so much as Osvaldo, I'm not so knowledgeable! (Maria-Grazia, first interview)

For Alessandra, the potential to learn was dependent on one's willingness to communicate in a reciprocal dialogic manner. As such it depended on the mindset of the participant as remarked on in the descriptions of their experiences of the debate group as communication:

> If you are open-minded then you probably still sometimes learn and teach others. (Alessandra, first interview)

> This sentiment was also reflected in Atena's comments that the debate group was a good place to come for people who want to share common interests in certain topics. (Atena, first interview)

Overall, however, such a situation was only successful, if the chair managed the discourse.

> This is the educational aspect, because if you (the chair – myself) don't manage the debate then it is only conversation. That's fine but we have to understand the topic, to develop the different aspects of the topic and this is the educational part. (Alessandra, first interview)

One part of this peer-led education was not only formed by learning factual knowledge from other participants but learning others' subjective views on topics:

> to understand the others' opinions ... each topic can give you new ideas and you can make a comparison between your ideas and the ideas of other people,

and this can activate your brain, your thinking, so I think it is very useful. (Alessandra, first interview)

In a similar sense, Maria-Grazia explained how the act of comparing ideas was also educational, suggesting that the willingness to debate is a way of transforming and challenging existing perspectives.

> I try to understand any difference that there are between my point of view and the point of view of other people. (Maria-Grazia, second interview)

These comments were expanded upon by many of the participants as contributing to positive affective affordances of the debate group, their experiences being mind-opening, promoting growth, promoting reflection:

> I think that there is a chance to increase your knowledge, your potential of thinking, seeing the world from another point of view if you are open minded. If you think you are always right (laughs) or you have a closed mind, then it's difficult to grow. (Alessandra, first interview)

> I can enrich myself ... learning about new things. (Laura, first interview)

Being open to reflect on ideas and opinions was also seen as a necessary aspect of the debate group as being educational:

> Of course, I come here to improve the language, but it is also an opportunity to change the opinions, to learn, and to learn from my fellow. (Salvatore, final interview)

On one occasion, the topic of whether euthanasia should be legalized was presented. Here, cultural awareness and educational objectives were highlighted. As attested by Valentina, though the topic certainly engaged the participants and we learned about each other's experiences, the debate centred more on the personal experiences of suffering in relation to family members as opposed to the legal question of assisted dying being addressed:

> Every one of us was reminded of a situation in their past that was unpleasant; this is a topic (euthanasia) that I don't think is to be recommended ... it was very strict and neat and the terms were clean and we had to respond in another clinical way. (Valentina, final interview)

Valentina suggested that had the debate been done in a different European country that possessed a lower level of emotional sensitivity to such topics, then it might have been possible to address it from the intended perspective, but that this was impossible in Italy.

The educational EFL dimension to the debate group

The second main part of the findings about the educational experience was shaped by the English language learning affordances of the debate group. As can be seen, much of this occurred autonomously, self-directed by the participants.

The communicative basis of the debates as speaking and listening was experienced as promoting the maintenance and learning of new EFL knowledge and language skills. This is crystalized in the following comment about Salvatore's motivation for joining the debate group:

> (I joined the debate group) for conversation because I needed comprehension and fluency. If you talk, the more you talk, the more you improve and the more you learn. (Salvatore, first interview)

Also typical is the autonomy in making notes during the debate, checking dictionaries or asking for the clarification of meanings of certain words:

> When I go home, I try to remember some things, new words, and I have a notepad and I note down the words, or I consult a dictionary and you extend the meaning of the words because words can have different meanings. (Salvatore, first interview)

Arturo explained the debate group possessed two main affordances for EFL:

> Talking and having debates forces you to think different things. One is to speak, and the other is to understand. And the sum of these two activities is best developed in debates. (Arturo, first interview)

He went on to say:

> (In a debate there) is a push to enlarge your capability your understanding of words you do not know. (Arturo, first interview)

Salvatore draws together the perspectives of the communicative and educational experience of topics by describing how the EFL element combines with them. The peer-led and self-directed learning skills as found in the group are once again evidenced:

> I also try to improve my English from who speaks English better than me, the comparison is a very good means to learn, not the competition, (but) the dialogue. (Salvatore, final interview)

Some other participants emphasized the concept of the debate group as also maintaining or recalling knowledge that they felt had been lost or was at risk of being forgotten through lack of use:

> I think it's ... a good method to improve a bit the language without too much commitment ... in reality I hope to improve a bit my English but not to lose it completely. (Valentina, first interview)

These comments can be contextualized by the fact that the participants are retired and see themselves at risk of losing such knowledge and communicative abilities. As such, debating helps to maintain a healthy mind and to remain connected.

> When I stopped working, I decided to come here just to keep my expertise and continue practicing English ... I do not expect to learn something but to keep the knowledge that I had. (Osvaldo, first interview)

> ... at my age it is easy to go downhill but when I have some curiosity, I take my mind alive. It's an important aspect for me and for my personality, because I also observe the difference between me and my school mates (her friends) ... for me its enrichment and psychological sustenance because I feel myself more or less present in the life of today. (Laura, second interview)

In the first group interview, several participants agreed that the debates were useful at promoting ability in conversation across a number of speech genres, including the type of interactions participants had while travelling abroad. What many of the participants felt was that they wanted me to intervene and correct their English. Some participants had stated in the one-to-one interviews that they enjoyed the fact that the debate group did not include this aspect, however so there was certainly not a unanimous consensus. I cautioned that a focus on the language could side-track from the debate, however they urged me to correct them. One suggested that I make notes and then at the end review them. I attempted to do this as far as possible during the remainder of the year.

The experiences related to the educational dimension also correspond to the basic binary of positive-negative affect as with the communicational dimension. Along these lines, the role of humanism in education seems significant for gaining an understanding of the affordances and challenges of a debate pedagogy as a means of teaching speaking in TEFL.

A cognitive experience

The cognitive experience of the debate group was discussed in relation mainly to the utilization of thought necessary for comprehension and articulation during the dialogue of the debates. The phrase 'a good exercise' was used by more than one participant to describe the following two goals: successful speaking and listening:

> When you are using it (English when speaking) in your mind then it is a good exercise ... but sometimes it is difficult for me when it is spoken fast. (Arturo, first interview)

> You can gain the ability to present your ideas because sometimes you know about a specific topic but it's not easy to explain your ideas to others, so this is a good exercise. (Alessandra, first Interview)

Atena remarked how she felt the need to 'rack her brain' to respond in debates. It was also stated that the debate group prompted thinking in a more general sense:

> It is a good way to listen and think. (Laura, First interview)

Debating was also reported as highlighting cognitive strengths and weaknesses of expression and comprehension, in part owing to the utilization of a foreign language. This same issue was mentioned by Alessandra in relation to the challenge of using a foreign language, as the means of expression, assuming of course that participants are thinking in Italian:

> ... you have the idea that sometimes you are not always saying what you want to say or expressing your ideas. Can you imagine if you have to do that in a second language? It is more difficult ... because sometimes I feel that I haven't used the exact words that give you my exact thoughts and this is because my capacity in Italian to express myself is greater ... this is a stressful problem. (Alessandra, first Interview)

The monitoring of others' EFL errors and comparing them to one's own as means of 'noticing' and improving language was also reported as a form of metacognitive-metalinguistic tool. Alessandra pointed out how listening for others' speech errors helped her become more conscious of what constituted correct and incorrect language:

> When the discussion is in a second language you can listen for errors in others' speech that I make but sometimes didn't realize. (Alessandra, first interview)

With respect to language output, Valentina reported how her use of metacognition helped her to try and become more creative with her language choices:

> I benefit from the linguistic point of view because I have to force myself to speak and to think about some words, verbs that I don't usually use. Sometimes there could be a word. For example, 'mismatch' I know what it means but I heard it recently and I realized that I couldn't use this word because I had almost

forgotten. And this happens with many phrasal verbs and things like this. So, it's effective ... (Valentina, first interview)

Although Arturo did not discuss any examples of cognition in action, he was able to demonstrate metalinguistic awareness of features of the language which he believed were part of the cause of his difficulty in comprehension:

> My purpose comes from my wanting to enlarge my ability of speaking English and also, I'd like to improve my capability of understanding fluent English, because English is made of basically bi-syllables and they are easily missed because of the phenomenon of weakening and then it's very easy to misunderstand. (Arturo, first interview)

Elsewhere, evidence was provided that the participants brought to the debate metalinguistic knowledge that informed their understanding of the challenges associated with operating in an EFL:

> English is different to Romance languages, so you have to think a bit more. (Valentina, first interview)

There appeared to be an awareness of a certain trade-off between accurate EFL and basic expression of thought in some participants. This represented a kind of communicative gap between thought and expression; the cause this time being that of employing English.

> I try not to use difficult words in the debate group. In the conversation group, I try to put into practice what I learn from my books because in the debates it's not so easy. I try to use an easier English to be clearer and to avoid saying something stupid. Of course, the topics are more challenging and of course, I feel more relaxed in the general English class. (Maria-Grazia, first Interview)

> Sometimes it is very difficult to realize because you have to think of the next thing you want to say and the tongue is disconnected from the brain sometimes. (Alessandra, first interview)

The participants' experiences of the debate group from a cognitive perspective appeared to mainly relate to the challenges of communication with respect to speaking and listening when dialogue is the main communicative process. On the other hand, it was reported that some aspects of the debate group – in comparison with some other types of ELT methods – and as reported in the feedback on communication – were less cognitively demanding:

> In the debate, it is easier than one-to-one lessons because your level of attention can be lowered or increased but you are always in the debate. (Alessandra, first interview)

Although Alessandra was the only participant who explicitly stated this in clear cognitive terms, it seems reasonable that the perspectives on this affordance of the debate group as a chiefly listening-based pedagogy.

The experiences of the cognitive dimension further draw upon the affective scale of positive-negative experience, though the negative experience has also been expressed as a positive form of stress that promotes the use of language-specific cognitive processes. In this sense, the definition of humanist experience is complicated. Nonetheless, humanism still can be seen to situate the participants' experiences within this educational context of speaking in TEFL.

A social experience

The debate group was also experienced as a way of socializing. In some cases, the reason for this was ascribed to the life stage of the participant:

> It's something I'm doing at the end of my professional life ... to meet people and have a good time ... I come here as a way of seeing friends. (Osvaldo, first interview)

Part of the initial motivation and ongoing attendance was cited as being based on the desire to interact with others on a social level, and not only by the necessity of needing people to debate with:

> I think that it is important for confrontation and relationships, I think it's important in our life to have relationships. (Maria-Grazia, first interview)

> I find myself in a good way in this group – comfortable – because there are good relations among everyone ... for me it is a comfortable moment when I come here for the debate. I feel first class (laughs) sorry, but it's my state of feeling, psychologically. (Laura, first Interview)

> It's my pleasure to come here and hear what my companions say. (Valentina, first interview)

This view was also shared by Salvatore:

> ... for me it's important some kind of socialization with other people. (Salvatore, final interview)

Salvatore approached me one week after the first interview to reiterate that he believed that there was a strong social dimension for him to the debate group. He said that getting to know each other, helped to build confidence in speaking due to the familiarity with others and that being participant in the debate group could contribute more when there is a sense of friendship in the group.

The positive social aspect was also expressed by others who remarked:

> I found it very friendly. (Maria-Grazia, first interview)

It was also described as:

> ... a good class with different people, and different personalities. (Alessandra, first interview)

This theme was also experienced positively in contrast with participants' experiences in other EFL contexts:

> I have not the sensation to come to school; to come here with some friends and hear their point of view, it's er ... less heavy and so I think this is good. (Valentina, first interview)

This 'softer' take on the debate group however should be considered alongside the prior comments that attribute a more serious and instrumental motivation to the debate group as an activity with a clear educational outcome. The data suggest that the social and indeed affective dimensions are inseparable for the participants.

Finally, it was also asserted that the mode of communication found in the debate group was important to learners. A comparison was made between the mode of an increasing amount of technologically driven socializing via social media and the face-to-face mode of the debate group:

> We are people who I think like to talk about matters, we like to see each other and give value to a discussion that is not performed on WhatsApp or social networks. (Osvaldo, first interview)

The social experiences of the debate group are perhaps the most clearly associated with those of affect, traditionally, and therefore the most obviously aligned within a humanistic account of education.

Chapter summary

This chapter has examined the findings of the interviews based on interview transcripts and interview notes according to the four themes identified. It has also illustrated the relational dynamics of the themes, demonstrating that the participant's experience comprises four experiences that are interdependent. Additionally, the definition and role of affect as a way of conceiving of experience has been presented that explains how it shapes the angle of the research and the way in which the participant's experiences can be considered. My commentary is based on reflective notes made immediately after each transcript was typed up and on further notes made during the analysis stage. The following 'Discussion' chapter will consider how the findings can be understood in relation – mainly – to two theoretical approaches relevant to the experiences of the language pedagogy thus described by participants. I will continue to – as has been repeatedly indicated – consider the various dimensions highlighted by participants – where appropriate – on a scale corresponding to their affective nature, through the philosophy of humanism applied to education.

8

Debating as a Process

In addition to the emergent themes that have been discussed in the previous chapter, the approaches to language teaching as found in Curran (1972) and Freire (1972, 1974) will be discussed to elucidate how the participant's experiences of the debate group can be understood. Both Curran (1972) and Freire (1972, 1974) share a concern for the experience of the learner, in particular in the context of teaching speaking a foreign language, while also seeking to understand experience from the humanistic perspective. My contention is that the key characteristics that the most recent large-scale research into EFL instruction have found are indeed also found in the debate pedagogy, i.e. that learners have the necessary time to engage in speaking, that the speaking is immersive, the topics are engaging and that it supports positive peer interaction (Thiriau et al., 2017). The only missing aspect with the specific debate pedagogy so far put forward is that supportive feedback is somewhat limited. However, in Chapter 10 I will present a modified and extended curriculum that ensures to provide that these considerations are met. It will also be suggested that the humanistic perspective provided via the themes of communication, education, cognition and the social that will be examined complement their theories. This will be followed by a consideration of how these insights can inform educational practice, what some of the limitations of the research are, ways in which the research could be disseminated and further ways in which future research could build on this study.

The following discussion of the four themes is shown to resemble parts of a process that it is suggested can produce further successive stages of simultaneous language and personal growth. For a preview of this as exemplified by the flow chart below (Figure 2).

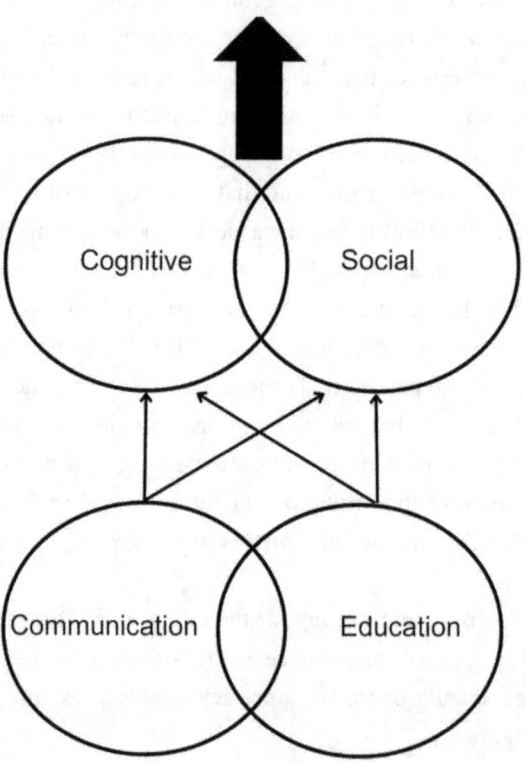

Figure 2 The process of debating.

The communicative experience

The personal challenge of debating

> I try not to use difficult words in the debate group. In the conversation group, I try to put into practice what I learn from my books, because in the debates it's not so easy. I try to use an easier English to be clearer and to avoid saying something stupid. Of course, the topics are more challenging and of course I feel more relaxed in the general English class. (Maria-Grazia, first interview)

Many of the participants' sense of debating as challenging, though, rewarding, can be associated with the aim to and fulfilment of higher needs and self-growth, and thus can be considered as a pursuit of humanistic needs through education. This was claimed to be unique to their experience of debating as a form of EFL education, and a positive affective experience, even if it was challenging. The concept which I previously discussed in relation to the humanism of Curran (1976) and Maslow (1999) involves the fulfilment of higher needs which in turn leads to self-growth. In humanistic psychology this is referred to as self-actualization and is described in a number of ways. Self-actualization is said to occur when we 'seek out new situations to master' (Glassman & Hadad, 2013, 276), such as those communicative situations, reportedly found in debating. As has been previously discussed in relation to Curran's counselling-learning theory (1972), evidence for debating as promoting higher needs can be seen in contexts in which speakers opt to partake in a communicative task that causes anxiety (Baran-Łucarz, 2014). While anxiety has been associated with restraining linguistic complexity in speech (Saslow et al., 2014), and reticence to engage (Liu & Jackson, 2011), from the perspective of affect it is also the first step to personal growth and self-actualizing; 'rather than representing a tranquil state of rest, self-actualization can be a painful process of struggle in order to grow. Because of this, we are driven to stretch ourselves, to reach new limits' (Glassman & Hadad, 2013, 276–7). As such, debating can be seen as a new situation to master. Indeed, in Vygotksian cultural historical approaches to psychology and learning, Vasilyuk argues that this is also an example of *Perezhivanie*, whereby it refers to 'the sense "to survive," that is, to pass through usually painful events, to overcome a difficult feeling, to endure, to maintain' (Vasilyuk in Meshcheryakova, 2016).

Debating as dialogue

The conception of the debate group as 'a chance to exchange' (Arturo, first interview) is largely the reason that the participants choose this type of language teaching context over others, as the findings demonstrated. What such a communicative exchange leads to – according to the findings – is a generally positive experience of language education, relative to the desires and autonomously identified learning needs. This was evident in the data, as Arturo explains:

> Exchanging your opinions with others is important because you communicate with them and, communicating is a way of enlarging your knowledge and offering your opinions to others, and therefore this enriches your way of living. So debating is important because it is a way of exchanging; it is a way of getting and offering as well. (Arturo, second interview)

Participants reported a positive affective experience of exchange, the term 'exchange' also signifying 'a giving and taking' (Arturo) which results in positive affective experiences by being 'interesting' and 'enriching'.

According to Freire (1972) – dialogue – and therefore exchange – is humanizing; whereas, it's opposite – what he terms 'the banking method', where learners are 'mere receptacles' deposited with information dictated by the teacher – is de-humanizing (Freire, 1972, 52–3). Dialogic speaking, according to Arturo and other participants, is characterized as cooperative instead of competitive, where terms such as 'exchange', 'offering' and 'getting' denote this particular form of verbal communication afforded by dialogue.

> For all parties, it makes the process in which they are jointly engaged more visible and explicit, valuing evidence and mutuality above supposition and gamesmanship.
>
> (Alexander, 2020)

Even though there remains a strong educational dimension in learning from each other as participants about factual knowledge, or when the learner provides their opinion, the affective outcome is only afforded by the way in which this knowledge is communicated and formed through verbal dialogue and therefore highlights this affordance of speaking. This also reflects what Curran (1972) argues about the learning relationship in adult humanistic pedagogy, as having entered a new paradigm, in which the debate group operates within the current communicative era of ELT history:

The student-learner and the teacher-knower can now be studied from a new point of view. In contrast to intellectualizing and actualizing, cognitive-affective and affective-cognitive expressions can be considered as the main means of communication. This, in fact, is what really does occur in any person-to-person involvement ... it is ... now evident-looking at humans as a unity-in learning experiences and relationships.

(Curran, 1972, 97)

Evidence of this new perspective on language teaching was made clear in the positive affect of dialogic teaching and the chance to exchange reported by participants which can be interpreted within Curran's (1972) notion of cognition and affect as being activated by communication through dialogue.

Because of the importance placed on serious communicative engagement demanded by speaking in a debate (Al-Mahrooqi & Tabakow, 2015), it provides an opportunity for deep expression and in turn, more challenging and engaging comprehension through listening. Debating, therefore, has the potential in foreign language teaching to involve the learner as a whole which promotes a positive affective experience, as it draws on the learner's values, convictions and experiences, also representing a communicative demand that is stimulating as much for cognition as for affect. This experience of learning from the humanist perspective of education suggests that debate pedagogy affords a potentially beneficial form of communication.

Redefining debating

I initially opened this book citing debate as 'in its broadest sense ... referring to a discussion in which individuals share their point of views on a given topic based on their experience and factual knowledge' (Al-asmari & Salahuddin, 2012). Debate may be more associated, however with the expression of subjective views that seek to persuade – and are therefore close to Aristotle's conception of Rhetoric (Aristotle, 2012). Socrates – before him – was explicit in differentiating between this kind of subjectivity and a dialectical approach to dialogue which instead involves the aim of seeking to establish truth between two or more sides through reasoned argumentation (Evangelidis, 2016). The participants, however, have redefined it. The participant's experience of the communicative dimension reports the debates as being more dialectal, but also as didactic, i.e. that participants experienced the debates as a learning experience. Now, a debate is not defined as either of these forms of dialogue, and yet for participants, their conception of their debating combines these two forms of communication.

Another way in which the initial conception of debate – common in Western society has been about – is competition. Instead, the kind of debate that took place in the debate group was not competitive at least in the sense that this was not its aim. Rather, participants objected to any sense that they were prevented from being able to contribute to the debate, due to some of the constraints that were outlined regarding time limitations, or owing to the challenges of using a second language. It is fundamental to bear this point in mind when approaching the suggestions for a pedagogy that follows: the literature and the specific research carried out by the author, in no way found that debate should be characterized as competitive, as far as the outcomes identified in the four categories of communication, education, cognition and the social are concerned. On the other hand, if the practitioner is familiar with their students and the group dynamics, and if they are keen to compete, then an alternative form of debating is possible. However, such a form of debate may differ quite markedly in terms of the experiences of the participant which should be borne in mind.

Listening and learner-space

Another facet of such democratic communication that was highly prized by participants was the relatively small amount of pressure to speak in the debates, and also in providing each participant a set time to speak so that the communication would not be interrupted and the speaker could express their thesis. This was evident in Osvaldo's comments regarding the change in the format of the debates, which gave each participant a set time in the beginning to speak, without interruption:

> I think that it was a very good thing to give time for everyone to speak. (Osvaldo, final interview)

In fact, until the turn-taking pedagogical shift was introduced, participants were not expected to contribute at all. The study found that this lack of pressure was appreciated by many, who said that one of the reasons that they favoured the language learning method of the debate group compared to conversation classes or on-to-one lessons was that they could focus on listening. This sense of liberty and security of not being forced to communicate can be seen as affective as each one has the freedom to express oneself or abstain; 'learners decide what to say and when to say it' (Stevick, 1990, 74); I, as the teacher-knower, merely pose the initial debate question and interject, only, to move the debate forward or to occasionally keep it on track. This reflects the affective management of the discourse, as found in Curran's counselling-learning approach whereby the greater the learners' sense of security, the more easily they are able to communicate when they feel comfortable to do so and focus on listening, also. This state of being is referred to as becoming 'Incarnate'. When motivation for the abstinence of speaking is such, it does not represent resistance to the experience of the debate but rather means that the participant at that moment is choosing to remain in the listening-comprehension-reflection mode, as opposed to the speaking-articulation-expression mode. As this form of communication in the debates promotes 'Incarnation', the students 'put more of themselves into the lesson (and) give it fuller attention' (Stevick, 1990, 76). The participants' experiences of learner-space therefore also indicate that the teacher has planned and taught, according to the student's learning preferences (Cambridge English, 2021, 2).

This communicative experience is certainly not a given in the two types of classes that the participants had experienced previously and expressly avoided for this reason. The debate model may also be seen in contrast to forms of English CLT which may perceive a willingness or low amount of student speaking to be evidence of a lack of engagement (Scrivener, 2005). In such contexts, the teacher may attempt to coax the learner into becoming involved against their wishes.

Although the debate group is not intended as ELT through direct instruction – my experience as the teacher and the knower of the target language was – nonetheless positioned by learners as the teacher who leads communication to some extent. However, in a potentially humanistic approach to education such as debating, the teacher-knower resists this traditional role.

> ... If the knower projects himself into (that) space, allowing no room in it for the learner, he destroys any opportunity for the learner to expand into it ... The learner continually moves closer to the 'target', the knowledge of the knower, until he reduces the knower to silence or 'nonexistence'. This is the final goal of learning.
>
> (Curran, 1972, 91–2)

The debate group pedagogy therefore also provides learner-space to participants through my minimal communicative intrusion. It is not the teacher's role to debate, and therefore their role should be one of only managing the dialogue when necessary, as a way of trying to increase the experience of the debates positively. During the debates, I only interjected to abide by the participant's wishes for me to keep the debate topic on track, and not to lecture or indeed provide my opinions or experiences unless specifically asked. Instead, it was my aim to foster a highly student-centred form of communication. I have increasingly been able to do this over the years as the participants have reached ever higher levels of independence regarding their language abilities and power of expression.

This hands-off approach to managing student communication can be interpreted as reflecting Curran's concept of the final 'death' stage of the learning trajectory, which simultaneously represents the relative communicative withdrawal of the teacher, contrasted with the ultimate level of educational attainment for the student as evidenced by their independence, i.e. the teacher-knower becomes increasingly peripheral as his or her support is less and less needed, and thus his initial more involved role has 'died' (1972) (Figure 2). This situation for the learner and the teacher means that the communicative objective of more independent speaking has been achieved. It is perhaps worth considering however that, Curran's theory of L2 development is not morally judgmental of the language ability of the learner, but rather of their willingness to try to communicate, even if their language is not of the same level as that of the highest level learners (stage five learners). Indeed, from this perspective, only an elementary level of the L2 is required in order to debate, as at this level a learner has acquired an adequate knowledge of the language to be able to discuss a topic, providing that they have some familiarity with it (Council of Europe, 2021).

Providing learner space through listening is experienced by learners as a humanistic potential of the model of education afforded by the debates. However, it is the communicative dynamic of dialogue which shapes this affordance, as each learner is given the opportunity to speak, and therefore to listen.

The act of listening as promoting mutual respect, tolerance and empathy

The concept of learner-space also relates to participants' positive experiences in their relations with fellow debate participants, which was described as fostering mutual respect, tolerance and empathy. This was related to respecting the individual characteristics of each other's foreign language skills, the pace at which they speak and the perceived quality of their contributions on the topic.

> Some people speak very quickly and have all their ideas just perfect, and another person is not so quick but their ideas are good in the same way. For example,

> student x sometimes speaks very fast and I have difficulty following him and he always says very interesting things. Student Y on the other hand is more slow but sometimes it seems that he has difficulties in speaking, but what he says is interesting too; so they have different ways of expressing their views. (Alessandra, first interview)

In part, this demonstration of respect can be seen as another facet of learner-space. Through exercising patience and a willingness to listen to others, learning can occur; clearly, it is only through a culture of dialogue that this can take place. Such experiences suggest that it is dialogue that produces this sense of humility. Also, from the perspective of expression, the data convey a sense of ease being felt.

> I could express myself because I was well. (Atena, second interview)

This situation reflects Curran's conception of a humanistic language pedagogy whereby the necessary community aspect of communication as,

> genuine communication that constitutes a community ... would be an open trustworthiness which is essential to one's freedom to communicate the participant's whole self in a group.
>
> (Curran, 1972, 30)

As such, even when the act of dialogue sometimes results in a difference of opinion, participants considered this kind of confrontation as a way of becoming aware of new points of view, and was considered positive, and a way of growing both intellectually and morally: in respecting each other their expression of themselves as people in the world and through communication becomes a part of it. For this type of EFL learner, therefore, the course, from a skills perspective, fulfils the participant's communicative motivation to both speak and listen. As such, this satisfies part of the humanistic criteria regarding the division of skills sought by participants, and secondly, the growth/self-actualization sought. This experience, therefore, evidences the requirement that the debates as language teaching pedagogy 'take into consideration learner's preferences and needs ... demonstrate language knowledge and awareness ... and are designed to develop the learners' overall language competence' (Cambridge English, 2021, 2).

These experiences also deepen the argument already made about the participant's communicative experiences being simultaneously cognitive and affective. This is noteworthy – as – more commonly, the language skills of speaking and listening in second language acquisition research, and indeed in foreign language research are generally viewed from a purely cognitive scientific perspective (Curran, 1972; Arnold, 2011; Dufva, 2013).

As with the previous account of learner space, debating, as a form of education, is clearly situated within a humanistic account that is shaped by dialogue as the main communicative dynamic.

The role of the teacher in managing communication and differentiation

Regarding the role of the teacher in managing communication and differentiation, the debate pedagogy was problematic at times and indeed was the only negative experience reported relating to dialogue. The issue related to my role in managing communication as the chair. During the first set of interviews, around half of the participants commented that they did not feel that they had enough uninterrupted time to speak. This was evidenced by Salvatore's comment:

> I want to add something but many times I can't succeed. (Salvatore, first interview)

This intrusion on learner-space was logically reported as having the opposite effect of the positive affordances that Curran argued for, i.e. that learner-space involves both removing the pressure to speak which is assumed to always be the main objective in CLT (Scrivener, 2005), and also ensuring that each participant is given the option to speak without interruption (Curran, 1972). It was suggested by one of the participants during their first interview that I intervene and re-structure the debate in a way that participants could be assigned individual time for a short introductory monologue. There was, therefore, a clear balance to be struck in trying to appeal to the humanistic concerns about turn-taking without going too far and overcompensating. If this could be achieved, then, my more active role would be humanizing, insofar as by structuring communication, the participant's aims are satisfied.

The participants succeeded in teaching me this, as previously I had possessed a more intellectualized notion of the role of the teacher. But my view corresponded to 'an intellectualized mode of learning (that) removes the teacher from any relationship with the learner, other than an abstractive intellectualized one' (Curran, 1972, 31). Instead, I became aware of the challenge to 'Incarnate' as the teacher-knower. If the teacher follows an intellectualized model of learning, then he or she prevents him or herself from becoming 'Incarnate', resisting the humanistic path to acknowledging his or her imperfections and dropping his or her 'mask'. In practice this means that the teacher prevents themselves from becoming a part of the community, opting instead to stay outside of it, by trying to retain a 'God-like' position over the group, thus resisting becoming 'Incarnate'. Given that my aims are to foster the participant's 'Incarnation', I, as the teacher-knower, must also have this as my aim (Curran, 1972).

Despite the appreciation of diverse language skills discussed earlier in relation to listening, a small number of participants perceived the diversity of language levels and communicative abilities as negative, insofar as it apparently impeded their experience of communicative flow. Specifically, participants felt that the relatively lower speaking abilities of some of the group impaired the overall quality of the debate. It was suggested that the responsibility was in my hands to 'compensate' for this lack of homogeneity, as was highlighted by Osvaldo by greater discourse management and correcting errors. From this perspective, the debate group is perceived as an ELT context in which learners should receive language instruction, in order to bring the lower-stage learners up to the level of articulation of the higher-stage learners. According to the data, the majority of the participants did not specifically state that this was the reason why they each wished to be corrected, however. I did re-cast non-target pronunciations, non-target vocabulary and grammar occasionally when learners looked to me to assist them. In general, however, 'warm, supportive, non-evaluative reflection' (Stevick, 1990, 75) based on participants' contributions was the main form of feedback provided. Indeed, both approaches to feedback related to monitoring language use reflect an important characteristic of the humanistic counselling-learning method (Curran, 1972).

On the other hand, the issue represents a major challenge for the teacher-knower, given that their aim as a humanistic teacher is to provide learner-space, which means not interrupting learners while they speak, and moreover not interrupting learners who have reached a stage of learning where correction can be met with hostility (Curran, 1972). Curran's description of the Five Stages of Language Learning can be seen to elucidate the reasons for these communicative conflicts, as the first four stages necessarily involve ever-decreasing support from the teacher until the fifth and final stages when they reach the stage of 'Independence'.

Based on the feedback of participants, it would appear that the group is divided into two sets. The first set of learners corresponds to the third 'Separate Existence' stage where the teacher-knower still provides words to the learner when they do not know them in English. Almost all of the participants, however, demonstrate that they are at the fourth 'Reversal' stage, in so far as they show concern for the teacher-knower, and therefore have begun to take on the advanced role of the learner as counsellor. This assertion is based on my experience as the teacher-knower-counsellor and reflects Curran's counselling-informed approach to language teaching, as he sees the learners becoming counsellors in their ascent towards improved language knowledge and use. In this sense they 'counsel' the teacher-knower in listening to them and giving them space to manage discourse through cooperation, and not through competition as was reported by some participants. This represents an important aspect of humanistic language teaching, which seeks to create a communicative context that is not based on tension and conflict, which can often occur when individuals are motivated by competition. Instead, an environment can be created in which through cooperation and mutual encouragement, equality is achieved. This is offered as a solution to overcoming the potential for student anxiety in a second language learning context (Curran, 1972), which can seriously impact progress in communicative ability (Arnaiz & Pérez-Luzardo, 2014).

According to Curran, if the participants do not do this, then the counsellor-knower will not feel comfortable enough to correct them (Curran, 1972). If the chosen model is relevant in this context, then the learners are indeed not homogeneous – as I – as the teacher-knower-counsellor – would supposedly feel more comfortable in correcting. I only clarified words when learners directly requested clarification which according to Curran represents the fourth stage of learning, and is crucial, if learners are to develop the language ability at the fifth and final stage of learning an additional language. Curran places this onus on the learner when they have reached this stage:

> The knower at this point is in need of being helped in his anxiety that he/she may be only causing pain and insult if he corrects the learners ... as the learner asserts his independent knowing-self, he must also open himself up to the knower, if he is to continue to learn.
>
> (Curran, 1972, 134)

Taking this into consideration, I would say that such a situation occurs due to my shortcoming as a teacher than that of the learners. This has been born of my very gradual learning of how to modify my teaching with the group whom I only saw once a week. In my mind, it is, therefore, unfortunate that a small number of the fifth 'Independent' stage participants feel disappointed about the abilities of the other participants. While they assume the positive counsellor characteristics often and support the lower-stage learners, their comments seem to express a certain degree of resentment over this role, accusing the learner-knowers of not fulfilling their role. In this sense the communal aspect of debating can be threatened by the resistance and unwillingness to 'die' for others, to use Curran's metaphor (Curran, 1972). In this sense, as Curran suggests, the counsellor-knower must be willing to make a 'selfless sacrifice'; a willingness to 'die' for the students to whom he is in service to. Indeed, it is my feeling that the priority is always to 'die' for each and every learner and 'sacrifice' myself by doing whatever it takes to ensure a positive experience of the debate. It is only then that the teacher can become fully 'Incarnate' as a humanistic teacher who promotes the debate as a holistic teaching method.

In defence of the 'Independent stage' participants, these findings suggest that it is not very humanistic to create language learning classes in which there is too great a diversity of language levels. Indeed, one solution suggested was for two debate groups to be formed (Alessandra, final interview), one with the 'Independent stage' learners and the other with 'Reversal stage' learners who still require some language support. The division created by the two sets of learners means there is friction between the two parties, making the experience of the 'Independent', final stage set of participants feel that the communicative process is hindered by a lack of ability to express – and therefore – also to be understood. While I did not feel as a partial observer that the communicative flow was sacrificed, this was clearly not the case according to the final stage group. While Curran views the inevitability of a mixed-level group being found in a language class as an opportunity for the participants to support one another – in this context – the opposite was found. As such, this humanistic potential in the act of peer support/scaffolding is experienced not as being humanistic and creates negative affective experience.

Another take on this situation is that those higher-stage learners who lament the lack of homogeneity – suggest – according to Curran – non-fulfilment of their roles as counsellors in the manner that I do. While they are willing to become 'Incarnate' as a learner, they are not necessarily as a counsellor – at least not in the sacrificial way that is required for the learner a counsellor (Curran, 1972). Perhaps, they do not recognize the overall educational benefits of this sacrifice, and as a result – by not accepting the other learners' lower abilities – they are actually not accepting their role as counsellors. In this way, they cannot become fully incarnate nor find reach the final stage of 'Redemption' through the educational process of the debate group. Indeed, it was the lower-stage group who spoke more directly about experiencing what Curran refers to as 'Incarnation', and indeed, the final personal growth stage of 'Redemption', perhaps, despite or due to their relatively lower listening and speaking abilities, they had more to risk, and took that risk of losing face, thus becoming 'Incarnate' learners (Curran, 1972).

The situation seems to also highlight the fact that there is a challenge in meeting all of the learners' needs. I am unwilling to correct and reconstruct what the 'Independent' group sees as being inadequately expressed arguments due to my employer's assertion that the group is not a traditional language lesson like the others that take place in the association and that in my view would certainly obstruct the communicative flow. On the other hand, the 'Independent' group sees this as one of two possible solutions to improving their negative experience of communication, the other being to create two separate classes. Though the teacher-knower has the moral intuition to respect the developmental process of the lower-stage learners, this can clearly have the side-effect of creating tension among the higher-stage learners.

Regarding their ability to communicate and express themselves effectively – the learners – according to Osvaldo are 'quite unequal', and this is experienced negatively. The essence of this concern can be seen as being experienced by all of the participants to some extent, in so far as the issue is about lack of language comprehension. This of course can be experienced by participants whose speaking ability is greater than others, and therefore feel frustration when they listen to other members who are not as articulate. However, the members whose English comprehension and speaking are lower feel frustrated when they do not understand the higher-ability students when they speak. Arturo provided a clear rationale as to why this issue was significant when he related the breakdown in communication caused by the apparent lack of skill in articulation having a negative impact on the level of educational attainment.

What debating highlights is that a perceived gap in communicative competence by some learners regarding others could be experienced as reducing the quality of the communicative experience. From Curran's perspective however, this relates ultimately to a non-humanistic, 'Incongruent' way of thinking whereby the participant prevents themselves from becoming 'Incarnate' and experiencing 'Redemption'; what he perceives to be the final goal. As can be seen, when a group of learners is not homogeneous, it highlights one of the challenges for language teachers when 'teaching and planning lessons which take account of learner's backgrounds, learning preferences, and current needs' (Cambridge English, 2021, 2). So, while I did endeavour to remedy this situation, demonstrating 'professional awareness and responsibility', I was still grappling with the complexity of this issue.

In conclusion, it is important to restate the prior caveat mentioned early on in this chapter, that there is not a perfect one-to-one fit between debating as conceived here as a method and counselling-learning as an approach. Rather, it is proposed that some general and more specific principles for informing those humanistic approaches to language teaching are pertinent; holistic approaches that consider both cognition and emotion, in relation to the development of L2 speaking as driven by dialogue and peer teaching. Both, it is proposed, are said to create an ideal pedagogy of teaching as learning and learning as teaching.

Aside from these immediate pedagogical concerns of debating, my role as practitioner-researcher in the research may have raised issues that would otherwise have been dealt with or approached differently by participants, and indeed by myself. While I am mindful of this as an issue, it is clearly not always possible to know exactly how the nature of my role has influenced the communicative experience. My positionality as a researcher – for example – could be influenced by cultural differences as a middle-aged English male, researching a group of Italian men and women – all at retirement age on the one hand, to more fluid, political, personal life history, subjective or other unidentified contextual factors (Holmes, 2020).

Despite some of the limitations outlined, this section has brought to the fore further contextual factors regarding the social actors involved in the context and demonstrated how the chosen humanist psychology, when applied to this model of education, can make clearer our understanding of learner experience.

The educational experience

Communication and curriculum design

The role of humanist psychology when applied to education is also fundamental in understanding the experience of education from the following experiences described by participants. In this first section, this concerns the role of curriculum design based on what interests the learners. Curriculum planning of topics that are based on learner interests reflects a humanistic philosophy of education, and the key to this is the process that takes place (Curran, 1972). The approach to curriculum design is based on my first year of chairing the group, in which the structure of the debates and the formulation of the topics were quite loose. The debate question was posed at the beginning of the debate, so participants had little time to prepare. Rather, they relied on higher-stage participants to elucidate the topic, which they then eventually built on. The eager that this new approach generated, combined with positive feedback about the pedagogical shift, convinced me to continue with it. Overall, however, the theme of the debate as an educational experience emphasized the experience of the debate to peer learn the English language learning dimension.

Fellow participants were seen to make a decisive contribution to the character of the educational dimension, and this was reported as one of the main factors that motivated participants to continue attending. The close connection between classroom communication and curriculum is considered fundamental by Freire who argues the curriculum should come from the students in dialogue with the teacher and each other (Freire, 1974). Therefore, the type of education enjoyed by the participants in the study would not be such, if the teacher took a more limited consideration of the student's interests, as found in a teacher-centred model of classroom talk. This approach can be seen to have generated a positive-affective experience of education, as pedagogy and curriculum combine to promote student roles that can be experienced as realizing higher needs or self-actualization as will be shown (Glassman & Hadad, 2013).

Though debating to some degree relies on subjective opinions and experiences, it was nonetheless made clear that there were some unwritten ground rules that should guide the calibre of the topics and how they were approached. Osvaldo, for example, contrasted his experience of the debate group with other forums that he was a member of:

> The most valuable thing … that's not common (is to) have discussions to a good cultural level. Discussions (can) go down to everyday matters or demagoguery or to unsubstantiated points of view, so the advantage for me is this. (Osvaldo, first interview)

The topics discussed by the group vary widely from 'What are the successes and failures of the baby-boomer generation?' 'Was the Technocratic government installed in 2011 a lost opportunity for Italian politics?' to 'Should voting in general elections be made compulsory?' These topics permitted the participants to draw on their life experience of having lived through many socio-political events over the past seventy years and to base their reflections in part on these experiences but also on the factual historical dimension. These topics were generated by the teacher-knower as chair, to initiate discussions based on topics that I had learned over time that were of interest to the participants. I learned of their interests by asking them what the general topics they were interested in were before the research even began. They explained that the previous chairs had autonomously selected debate questions and that they wished to continue with this format. In order to inform my choices, I engaged in a brief conversation with the group before the debates in which they would frequently be discussing current affairs. With the accrual of these topics, I was able to build up an ever deeper and broader knowledge of what interested them. This approach provided topics that formed the basis for 'engaging in real conversation … in a foreign language, a humanistic I-myself engagement' (Curran, 1972, 129), thus leading to the student reaching the state of 'Incarnation' (Curran, 1978). In this way, the learner becomes a learner-knower as they dare to communicate and express themselves (Curran, 1972). This is one way in which the curriculum can be seen as being humanistic.

It is owing to this approach, whereby the teacher engages in dialogue from the very beginning of a course that a collaborative curriculum can be formulated. Freire refers to such a knowledge base as the 'Thematic Universe' from which the curriculum is not preconceived as an 'elaborate itinerary' starting from points the teacher has pre-determined (Freire, 1972, 89); rather that it is grounded in the students' histories. As the teacher-knower, I only briefly presented the topic, from which participants then set about learning both autonomously and collaboratively – researching and reflecting on the topic and then formulating their views. In the following debate which would take place one week later – the participants – without interference – express their views:

> The students – no longer docile listeners are now critical co-investigators in dialogue with the teacher. The teacher presents the material to the students for their consideration and re-considers his or her earlier consideration as the students express their own.
>
> (Freire, 1972, 62)

The approach to curriculum described is humanistic as it prioritizes students' interests and unfolds in an organic way, instead of those of a pre-planned, one-size fits all model as found in a number of adult EFL contexts. The teacher looks to the learners as an initial 'text' from which to then choose a specific topic to debate. As time goes by, the teacher discovers more about the learner's Thematic Universe and the learners continually deepen their exploration of these motivating topics which have the potential to promote self-growth/actualization (Freire, 1972, 1974). As conceived by Curran (1972), such topics also afford the kind of foreign language speaking that fosters self-actualization which is considered to develop a learner's speaking ability towards the desired final level in which they are independent of the teacher (Curran, 1972). Again, curriculum content, when derived through the teacher listening to learners' discussions, is motivated by humanistic concerns, because of the fact that it seeks to engage learners instead of disregarding their interests (Freire, 1972, 1974).

Topics

Similarly, the specific topics that I selected for each debate – though not specifically chosen by participants – were still chosen based on the same humanistic stance of education reported throughout this thesis.

In part, due to the reported intellectual and critical thinking that the topics inspired, they were also experienced as being engaging and promoting argumentative discussion. The evidence, therefore, suggests that learner needs were assessed, and lessons were taught and planned that took into ' … account learner's backgrounds, learning preferences and current needs' (Cambridge English, 2021, 10), 'language knowledge and awareness, and appropriate teaching strategies' were employed and that 'knowledge about language skills and how they may be acquired' was ensured to some degree:

> In my opinion, you learn more in the debate because many times there are topics that interest you. The interest in a matter is fundamental. If you have limited interest in a matter, you learn a limited amount. (Arturo, first interview)

> I have learned about subjects that previously I could have much interest in and so this is an enrichment in my view. (Laura, second interview)

This was contrasted with participants' other experiences with – for example – one-to-one or conversation lessons which were reported as lacking such depth. The relatively safe and superficial idealized nature of the topics that participants had experienced in other contexts is described by Curran (1972) as being 'Discarnate'. The data show how the participants preferred non-idealized topics which required encountering the challenging issues facing society. Curran refers to these topics as fostering the learners to become 'Incarnate' as they unify the 'I' (which represents the egocentric self that seeks to not lose face) with the 'Myself' (which represents the self that takes those risks), resulting in the 'Incarnation' of the learner. This occurs by learners accepting their learner-self that might make mistakes and errors then being challenged and rising to these challenges. The type of pedagogy found in the debate group invites the participant to engage with real-world topics at a time in their lives when they may feel a sense of disconnection due to retirement (an issue that will be discussed in relation to the social experience). Such an activity can be considered humanistic because participants become authentic by being engaged in enquiry and creative transformation.

> Problem-posing education bases itself on creating and stimulates true-reflection ... thereby responding to the vocation of persons as beings who are authentic only when engaged in inquiry and creative transformation.
>
> (Freire, 1972, 65)

It is important here, to highlight the distinction between a discussion about a topic in a conversation class that some of the participants referred to having experienced, with the sustained mining of the 'Thematic Universe' which the teacher-knower over time has tapped into, and fostered the continuing emergence of: This was evident in the data, as conveyed here, by Salvatore:

> In a private one-to-one lesson, it is only for the language, so you are less motivated. And when we (and his former teacher) talked in a very free way the topic was very limited; life, your family, your work; once, twice then it's very boring. The debate group engages you. (Salvatore, first interview)

The topics accessed in debating, therefore, relate to human aspirations, motives and objectives; and are not just light-hearted, occasional exchanges, as reported by Salvatore. This view of learning also reflects Curran's whole-person model – whereby a humanistic pedagogy necessarily draws on an equal engagement of cognition and emotion, as creating humanistic education. Clearly, this cannot take place when the curriculum is viewed as a separate, objective phenomenon that does not truly relate to the learner's lives (Curran, 1972), and, thus, contributes to the argument for a humanistic pedagogical approach as advocated by this study.

That this occurs in the debate group can also be seen in the participant's reported continuing research on what has been discussed after the debate (Valentina, second interview; Laura, second interview) as the debate topic can be 'consumed' by the participants across three prolonged stages: Firstly, the pre-debate research on the topic, then the peer-learning and sharing of knowledge and perspectives during the debate, followed by post-research stimulated by new information discovered in the debate that participants wish to research further (Valentina, second interview; Laura, Second interview). In this way, the topics and participants' views do not remain 'out there' (Freire, 1972, 88) but are worked on, and internalized individually and communally. Interestingly, the development of the pedagogy which we achieved mutually through my setting the topic the week before, to give participants the chance to read up on the topic – then post-debate engage in further reading about the topic – begins to resemble the approach taken in TBL (see Chapter 2). Indeed, Chapter 10 provides a significantly developed curriculum and pedagogy, inspired by these aspects of the pedagogic shift that were informed by both myself a as practitioner and participants. These amendments were therefore motivated by a reflexive process and further motivated students to increase engagement.

Cultural awareness in topic selection

This experience of education highlights the need for awareness of the local cultural context within the broader stance of humanism and education. Although the debates were experienced as engaging, this does not mean that they were always positively engaging. One participant pointed out that one of the most memorable debates for her was the debate about whether euthanasia should be legalized in Italy. This was evident in the data, as evidenced Valentina:

> Every one of us was reminded of a situation in our past that was unpleasant; this is a topic (euthanasia) that I don't think is to be recommended … it was very strict and neat and the terms were clean and we had to respond in another clinical way. (Valentina, final interview)

Here, the issue of cultural awareness and educational objectives were highlighted. As attested by Valentina, though the topic certainly engaged the participants and we learned about each other's experiences, the debate centred more on the personal experiences of suffering in relation to the illnesses of family members, as opposed to the legal question of assisted dying. This occasion illustrated how the curriculum could cause distress, and in this specific context – given their life experience of the death of close family – to all members of the group. Valentina suggested that the fact that the participants were not able to discuss the topic in a detached manner was probably due to the participants' Italian culture and that if the same topic had been posed in Sweden, then it would probably not have caused such upset. My lack of cultural awareness was regrettable, but fortunately, this was an isolated episode. Cultural sensitivity and awareness regarding the selection of topics are therefore fundamental in creating a positive-affective educational experience, and a close engagement with participants' culture is fundamental in creating this understanding (Freire, 1974).

The dynamics of peer learning

The dynamics of peer learning reported by participants highlight the importance for teachers to observe and enquire into them, in order to improve any difficulties experienced by learners that could, by being overcome, improve learning outcomes, and increase positive experience. This is another fundamental consideration as far as a humanistic stance on education is concerned, as it seeks to promote well-being.

> When we talk about history, politics, and social events, you acquire knowledge. For example, Osvaldo is quite educated and knowledgeable about history and science. I have learned many things from him and Arturo, and Alessandra and their experiences in other countries. (Salvatore, first interview)

While participants reported that they had learned a great deal of factual knowledge about history and science in the debates – at no point was it reported that the learners had learned anything about the English language from the teacher; the occasional corrections and input via the teacher speaking were apparently of little importance.

> You don't come here to study language, you come here to have an exchange of opinion. (Valentina, first interview)

Despite this perspective, the learners still attested to the role of myself as the chair as fundamental in structuring the debate, so that it remained educational, as has already been pointed out in relation to the communicative experience. It is also interesting that here learning is related to the learning of factual knowledge about the topics and not the English language per se. However, according to the SLA research – already discussed – this doubtless occurs, as a consequence of exposure and use of the target foreign language. As has been previously outlined, this is known as 'incidental learning' (Whong, 2011).

That learning takes place in such a non-traditional non-hierarchical manner suggests that the group has reached the Independence stage described by Curran (1972), and that their experience is not that of traditional language students who focus more on studying language. Rather, they focus on using it:

> Stage V (five) is that of final independence of the learner from the knower. At the end of this stage the learner theoretically knows all that the knower has to teach. But although the stage V learner is, in fact, independent, he or she may still need some subtle linguistic refinements and corrections. He or she also gains much from the silent convalidation of the mimetic expert. The student in Stage V can become a counsellor to the other less advanced learners. In this way the learner progresses from client-learner to counsellor-knower-learner to expert-knower. As he or she counsels embryonic learners in Stages I, II and III, he can still, at the same time, receive subtle improvements from the language expert, who, for the most part, is a silent but important convalidating presence. His or her silence attests to the learner-knower's correctness.
>
> (Curran, 1972, 134)

Although this description does not exactly mirror the experiences of the learners, it nonetheless provides an approximate scale and description of peer education in the debates. The transformation of the learner as a counsellor does occur both from the perspective of the higher stage students providing language knowledge and factual knowledge related to the topics. Despite this emphasis on the important role of peer learning, Curran maintains that the learners continue to seek the linguistic knowledge of the knower (myself the chair) until 'reaching a state where they no longer need him or her' (Curran, 1972, 140). Moreover, as Curran asserts, the silence of the teacher is evidence of the learner-knowers language achievement, thus demonstrating that the debate pedagogy is not one of typical transmissive teacher-centred learning.

Given that not all learners are at the same learning stage in the debate group, this reliance on the knower persists even if to only a degree; on the one hand to provide knowledge of language where there are gaps in communication, which I did, and on the other as an intermediary who manages communication so that the educational goals are met. All the while however, according to participants – the teacher-knower rarely imparts factual knowledge or opinion, nor teaches language in the traditional sense – but rather facilitates the debates; as was evidenced in my role being referred to as that of a 'safety net' (Atena, first interview). Curran refers to this relationship between knower and learner as mimetic, as the knower seeks to 'eventually give up his power (and has) died in a sense-so that the learner, now knower, can live independent from him' (1972, 140). Furthermore, for Curran, this seemingly narrow or reduced language teaching role is nevertheless still language teaching; the caveat being that it is a form of language teaching based on the teacher's understanding of their role in the long-term diachronic learning trajectory, as captured by the Five Stages Theory (Curran, 1972).

This approach to teaching and learning can be seen as humanistic, as it prioritizes the role of the student to be transformed into that of a teacher, thus indicating that this skill is being used or that it has been learned thanks to the affordances of debating. It does not limit the potential of the learner by limiting their role but rather promotes the inherent abilities of each participant to learn and teach. Depending on the goals of the participant, this could also indicate the attainment of self-actualization which within Maslow's hierarchy of needs (Maslow, 1999) represents that of a higher need. The teacher promotes this horizontal form of education as a way of maximizing self-actualization and growth. It is not enough for the student to only grow through learning the language and about topics, but to also teach the topics. A teacher-centred approach cannot permit this kind of growth, as the roles are non-negotiable: 'the teacher knows, and the students learn from the knower' (Freire, 1972). The language learning stages of the participants mean that they have surpassed this traditional model, and therefore, cannot allow them to flourish as the debate method does. Debating, therefore, promotes a positive experience of the educational experience which can also be described as humanistic according to its potential to stimulate personal growth.

Indeed, based on the learner interviews it appears that individually the learner's interaction does reflect these learning stages, and that my role as the teacher-knower had begun more and more to resemble the one described in stage five of Curran's scale (Curran, 1972). This aspect of the research, however, is a diachronic phenomenon that can only be captured in longitudinal research. It is only through managing classroom communication during the debates – a basic and fundamental requirement of the teacher in language education – that he or she is needed by the group to ensure that positive affective experience of debating as a way of teaching speaking is maintained. In this sense, the teacher is truly counselling them as Curran argues (1972) – insofar as the teacher is trying to stimulate positive communication between the members, with the aim of fostering individual well-being through group communication. Such dynamics can be clearly accounted for by a humanistic stance on education, as it prioritizes understanding of the dimensions of education, and how they are experienced, so as to potentially ameliorate them.

The EFL learning dimension

The theme of education from the specific perspective of EFL learning can also be related to the role of affect in Curran's learning stages discussed previously. It seems that in both the group and individual interviews, what was being reflected was what one participant had surmised about the group being divided in two with respect to speaking competence.

> We are quite unequal; we are not homogeneous in this we are quite differentiated and some trail behind the others quite a lot. (Osvaldo, final interview)

This comment reflects a negative experience of debating and was shared by others. While around half of the group are stage five 'Independent' learners, requiring only very occasional linguistic support, the other three would require the kind of support found in earlier stages. This issue impacted the English language learning educational experience, where many of the participants felt that they wanted me to correct their English during the debates. As previously discussed, some participants had stated in the one-to-one interviews that they enjoyed the fact that the debate group did not include this aspect, however, so there was certainly not a unanimous consensus. In one of the focus group interviews, we discussed this issue and I cautioned that a focus on the language could side-track from the debate. However, many participants urged me to correct them. One suggested that I make notes on their language errors and then at the end of the debate and review them. Such errors were rare, however, and based on my education as an English teacher, never impeded communication. I explained that the debate group was not designed to focus on this kind of education and that the policy of the school's management as a policymaker, and my knowledge of the aims of debating in the ELT literature, was to focus on fluency (Hunter, 2012). Indeed, it has been found that avoiding teacher correction in dialogic speaking practices affords the development of fluency and language complexity (Hunter, 2012). Moreover, debating as a pedagogy clearly emphasizes fluency over accuracy (Aclan & Aziz, 2015), and it is primarily for this that participants attend the debates, as evidenced in their one-to-one interviews. Nonetheless, I stated that I would endeavour to correct them as long as my correction would not disrupt the flow of the debate, as after all, I was investigating learner experience, and open to ameliorating the pedagogy as stated in the methodology.

The expectations of participants in relation to this aspect of the educational experience highlight an important tension, which in order for the debates to be experienced more positively – according to the independent-level learners – would require a radical separation of the group into two separate classes. Their expectations could also reflect participants' experiences of other dominant pedagogical approaches, and thus it is interesting to consider learner expectations when arguing for alternative pedagogical approaches such as that of employing debating. In addition, there is an expectation for the language teacher 'to develop their learner's overall language competence' (Cambridge English, 2021, 2), the correction being one such way of meeting this need. This aspect of the teacher assessment criteria could therefore be considered to be a humanistic consideration, insofar as correction as a form of language development is a given, and when not provided, denies learners the opportunity to 'teach lessons that take into account learners' needs, and indeed, was the cause of disappointment on the part of learners when I did not correct them, according to the focus group feedback. Such a consideration is also reflected in teacher training, whereby a teacher is expected to teach a variety of speaking lessons that range from a focus on accuracy to a focus on fluency (Scrivener, 2005; Cambridge English, 2021).

This tension was presumably created by a lack of mutual understanding between the participants and the school's policy, that the chair does not have any responsibility to teach language during the debates. As such, my rationale for not radically changing my approach was partly based on the internal pedagogical policy of the school that limits my independence to make decisions about pedagogy along with my responsibility. However, professional and responsible decision-making is a duty assigned to the language teacher (Cambridge English, 2021). As such, this highlights a tension between the educational policymaker, the teacher and the students as the three stakeholders found in educational contexts.

The second main part of the findings about the educational experience was shaped by the English language learning affordances of the debate group. More specifically, the communicative basis of the debates as speaking and listening was experienced as promoting the maintenance and learning of new EFL knowledge and language skills. This is crystalized in the following comment about Salvatore's motivation for joining the debate group:

> (I joined the debate group) for conversation because I needed comprehension and fluency. If you talk, the more you talk, the more you improve and the more you learn. (Salvatore, first interview)

For stage 3–5 learners, it is the opportunity to converse and listen in the L2 that is most fundamental for increasing fluency from their perspective and indeed is a major affordance of dialogic speaking as found in debating (Hunter, 2012). It is, therefore, not surprising that the participants were highly motivated by the educational aspect of the debate group. It is through praxis that the learners feel that they were achieving and that they were engaging with the language. This contrasts with a teacher-centred pedagogical approach in which student speaking time is more limited due to the emphasis on studying grammar and vocabulary (Curran, 1972). Participants were also actively engaged as they autonomously made notes of the new language and often checked their dictionaries for definitions of words. The debate group as a speaking task also affords an engagement with wider aspects of literacy, as participants read articles and books in English about the topics, before and after each debate. This was attested in the interviews and has been evidenced as an affordance of debating in TEFL (Aclan & Aziz, 2015) as an important aspect of the debates that showed how – beyond occasional conferring with participants for word meanings when needed – frontal teaching of language was unnecessary and only required very occasionally. This method also appeals to those who partake in the debate group as a means of recalling language that they perhaps have forgotten or fear that they may lose, by having the opportunity to speak and thus mentally searching for words to express themselves. The focus remains on language-use, which highlights gaps in knowledge that are semantically pertinent to the topics, which can then be filled by looking them up; the most effective way a new language can be learned (Kebler, Liebner, & Mansouri, 2011).

With regard to my positionality as researcher-practitioner in this exploration of the educational experience of the debate group, my role revealed how my practices as a teacher became more visible for both myself and the participants, and that the two roles are inseparable (Holmes, 2020). I exposed the extent of my power regarding choices of what to teach, even if based on attempts to consult with participants. Given my added role as a researcher, I also left myself vulnerable to criticism. However, this criticism was aimed more at the communicative aspect of my practice, despite the concerns raised by participants regarding correction. These issues can be seen to have revealed some of the contextual tensions created by my dual role, and the way in which it shapes my positionality as a researcher (Holmes, 2020).

A cognitive experience

Introduction

Although cognition is often treated as a purely objective scientific phenomenon, the experiences of participants through the humanistic stance on education reveal how subjective experience of cognitive processes can play an important role in speaking in a foreign language.

Both communication and education as conceived thus far, necessarily involve cognition. Two main issues emerged from the data involving this dimension: firstly, the stress experienced through cognitive processing of language and thought (Baran-Łucarz, 2014; Saslow et al., 2014), and secondly, the role of metacognition that can be utilized during speaking (Ganem-Gutiérrez & Nogués-Mélendez, 2013).

> … you have the idea that sometimes you are not always saying what you want to say or expressing your ideas. Can you imagine if you have to do that in a second language? It is more difficult … because sometimes I feel that I haven't used the exact words that give you my exact thoughts and this is because my capacity in Italian to express myself is greater … this is a stressful problem.
>
> (Alessandra, first interview)

Though characterized as 'a stressful problem' by Alessandra at the affective level, her description of the communicative dimension of debating is supportive of research that shows that such cognitive challenges positively influence second language acquisition (Whong, 2011). Indeed, according to Curran (1972), these negative experiences can be transformed into positive, ones when the learner is made aware of the developmental significance of experiencing such challenges both on the personal level and the cognitive.

Speaking and listening, and anxiety

It is from the perspective of anxiety that we can claim that the cognitive dimension – as reported by participants – provides evidence of affective experience which regarding the interests of the research, corresponds to an evaluation of the debate group as humanistic pedagogy. Any challenges experienced by participants in the debate group regarding cognition can be seen to relate to individual efforts to comprehend or express. When a participant describes the experience of employing such skills, this can be taken as evidence of engagement in either listening or speaking in the debate. The question then arises as to how this engagement, whether low or high, stressful or relaxing is experienced. The cognitive processing in speaking (Saslow et al., 2014). and listening (Elkhafaifi, 2005) associated with expression as sensory-motor skills is, however, influenced by anxiety.

Some participants partly attributed cognitive stress to the added pressure of using their L2 (English) as the mode of expression. This was reported as being of two kinds; one influenced by the processing and organizing of ideas and opinions, the other being the challenge in the L2 of expressing these ideas when there are gaps in their knowledge of grammar, vocabulary or pronunciation. Indeed, such anxiety has been identified as being caused by the speaker's self-imposed attention to accuracy (Baran-Lucarz, 2014; Saslow et al., 2014; Meigouni & Shirkani, 2020). The debate group participant's interviews showed that the cognitive stress apparently caused by having to express thought in the L2 can be such that some participants feel they must simplify their language in order to be able to articulate their ideas. Indeed, stress has been correlated with low linguistic complexity when speaking one's first language (Saslow et al., 2014) and the second (Khan, 2010). There is certainly a communicative challenge associated with the complexity of language required in debating (Freely & Steinberg, 2014), and such challenges are experienced more generally in CLT dialogic speaking (Arnaiz & Pérez-Luzardo, 2014; Baran-Łucarz, 2014;

Pishghadam, 2016; Toubot et al., 2018; Setiawan, 2018; Liu & Xiangming, 2019; Meigouni & Shirkani, 2020). It also showed that there was a perceived disadvantage to this, as participants sometimes felt that what they said was not expressed in the same articulate manner as they are capable of when not under pressure. In this sense, some participants experienced a reduced level of satisfaction with their communication at times. This is one area of the debate group that due to such pressure – given the necessary linguistics skills required – can lead to a lowering of positive affect. However, instead of being detrimental to learning, such a challenge can simultaneously be considered to be indicative of the cognitive engagement necessary to learn (Curran, 1972) and furthermore to self-actualize (Curran, 1972; Glassman & Hadad, 2013). Therefore, instead of serving as evidence of this representing a deficiency of debating in the debate group, it could be evidence of and promote a teacher to 'demonstrate language knowledge and awareness, and appropriate teaching strategies' (Cambridge English, 2021, 2).

The situation represents an interesting trade-off that I would argue is entirely acceptable and expected. Indeed, in the contemporary literature on the relationship between stress and speaking, there is the suggestion that speaking is often experienced negatively, when not managed sufficiently by the teacher. However, such studies are not longitudinal and therefore do not capture the five stages of learning that Curran (1972) argues is fundamental in understanding the necessary evolution of the learner. This is to say, that the learner has the potential – through the personal growth process of becoming 'Incarnate' – to improve their speaking abilities (Curran, 1972). Indeed, this book has identified and considered the applicability of these stages; what is important from a humanistic stance is that such struggles – by the end of each debate – and indeed over the years in which the participants have been attending the debates – result in a positive educational experience. This can be viewed as an example of what Stevick highlights in Curran's concept of 'Redemption' (1978). The teacher as 'the other' in the student-teacher 'I-myself-other' (Curran, 1972) relationship invites the student into a situation (the debate) where the teacher knows that the student may experience some stress. However, this is why the learner must also unify themselves, not only with their 'I-myself' but also with the teacher-knower thus forming a 'I-myself-other' relationship:

> … the redemptive relationship with the other … is a very caring concerned regard for the real self, the best self. It confronts the 'myself' in those stages that are impeding the best self.
>
> (Curran, 1976, 24; Stevick, 1990, 82)

Stevick further elaborates on Curran's conception of this relationship:

> Curran often compared the role a 'redemptive' or therapeutic 'other' to that of a dentist, who does not passively 'accept' a patient's teeth as they are but works to make them the best they can become even at the cost of some temporary pain to the patient.
>
> (Stevick, 1990, 82)

Stress, in this situation, may highlight a challenge for the participant that could potentially be strengthened through practice in speaking and listening under positive, humanistic conditions (Curran, 1972; Curran, 1978). Indeed, language teachers have been implicated as the source of anxiety (Han et al., 2016; Effiong, 2015) and speaking as causing anxiety (Arnaiz & Pérez-Luzardo, 2014), thus reflecting the potential of speaking to cause anxiety in the ways highlighted in Curran's counselling-learning theory. Furthermore, practising this challenging skill has also been found to reduce anxiety by facing up to it (Tridinanti, 2018), as advocated by Curran (Stevick, 1990). Additionally, learner attitude has been implicated as a significant barrier to reducing speaking anxiety (Buriro & Siddique, 2015). This suggests that there are a number of complex factors that contribute to these challenges faced by learners and that the kind of dynamics described by Curran (1972) is accurate.

Taking into consideration the experiences of both speaking and listening in relation to cognition, both the pressures that are present when learners choose to engage in verbal communication are there to help promote language learning, yet in the same context they can work on their comprehension and grammar and vocabulary building. These options available to learners, in themselves could be seen as offering a humanistic method, as learners are able to work with some autonomy, self-directing their learning within the debate. This may be less likely found in many other contexts where there is less flexibility in approaches to language learning and curriculum, as the aforementioned research into contemporary speaking in EFL suggests.

To address these issues as they became apparent in the debate group, there were a number of ways, however, during the year in which the interviews were undertaken, a pedagogical shift, based on this feedback was carried out to reduce this stress at the level of comprehension and expression. This involved a restructuring of the staging of the debates as described (Table 2). Learners were each provided with five uninterrupted minutes in which to put forward their response to the debate question which had been posed at the end of the previous debate. After which, a freer debate would ensue in which participants could comment and build on each other's views. Though externally this is manifested by re-working the lesson plan as external communication, it has the collateral effect of re-structuring individual approaches to speaking and listening, given that – in theory – the cognitive load concerned with both aspects of sensory-motor concerned. This was reported by participants in their appreciation of having time to prepare for the debates a week in advance, and by being allocated time to speak and to listen without interjection. This has been found to be useful for students, as attested by Aclan & Aziz, (2015) and Al-Mahrooqi & Tabakow, (2015). Both found that advanced preparation afforded a deeper engagement with the topic, and that assignment of speaking time improved communicative efficacy. The restructuring of the debates which provided learners with preparation time before the debate, more reflection time during the debates, and time between the following debates to review and reinforce learning of new language could be ways of supporting and reducing the stress in processing and fostering the utilization of metacognitive strategies for improving language learning. These measures also reflect the language teaching assessment guidelines whereby teachers are expected to 'plan and prepare lessons designed to develop their learners' overall language competence' (Cambridge English, 2021, 2).

Curran (1972) provides an interesting synthesis of how these cognitive-linguistic aspects of foreign language learning classes experienced by the learners are not experienced as a purely cognitive phenomenon. Rather, there is a necessary interface with the social and therefore the affective. The kind of foreign language model proposed:

> ... sharpens, the awareness of the community side of mutual engagement and belonging that is so rich in the motivation of learning, but also emphasizes the learning side, which, in a non-personal way is expressed by laws of grammar, universally and commonly accepted vocabulary, and various subtleties of style and expression.
>
> (Curran, 1972, 33)

The concern with language – in a communicative, dialogic language learning form of education – necessarily 'forces the self of the learner out of themselves, if they wish to genuinely communicate with others, which is essential to being in true community with them' (Curran, 1972, 33). In this way, the experience of individual cognitive stress concerned with the processing of a second language in a communal, social, communicative context can be seen as being also connected to the social experience; an issue that I will eventually address. The humanistic stance on education has revealed learners' experiences that explain the kind of challenges that can occur for learners and teachers, in communicative management that would not otherwise be likely to emerge, and that therefore could go unaddressed. As such, this form of enquiry is asserted to be fundamental for increasing the efficacy of the teaching of speaking and the experiences of learner and teacher.

The role of metacognition in foreign language learning and language use

The following cognitive experience demonstrates further, how, though cognition offers an account of cognitive processes, the emotional experience of these processes in the context of education can provide a far greater understanding and appreciation of what is like to be a language learner in the classroom, and therefore how the teacher can attune their pedagogy to the challenges experienced by learners. This represents a humanistic stance on education, as it is concerned with the emotional experience, and not just the technicalities of acquisition as per linguistic processing in isolation (Arnold, 2011).

There is growing evidence to suggest that the role of metacognition offers a powerful tool for both students and teachers to enhance learning across all educational contexts (OECD, 2021), in relation to language teaching and learning (Roher & Ganem-Guitérrez, 2013), and more specifically teaching speaking (Ganem-Guitérrez & Nogués-Meléndez, 2013). There are a number of theories that serve to clarify and elucidate the debate group participant's experience of employing conscious formal knowledge of grammar and vocabulary to support their performance in speaking. Each of which will be discussed.

Another significant aspect of the cognitive experience was related to language awareness. More specifically this is termed 'metalinguistic knowledge' as a form of metacognitive awareness. The data recount how some participants employ metacognitive strategies when speaking and listening. They report using their knowledge of language systems (grammar) to receive the language input that occurs in the debate and analyse it as a means of improving their L2 knowledge, and then their use of the language. The process also involves noticing gaps in language knowledge and consciously searching their vocabulary for the correct target language to fill in these gaps.

> I benefit from the linguistic point of view because I have to force myself to speak and to think about some words, verbs that I don't usually use. Sometimes for example there could be a word. For example, 'mismatch' I know what it means but I heard it recently and I realized that I couldn't use this word because I had

almost forgotten. And this happens with many phrasal verbs and things like this. So, it's effective ... (Valentina, first interview)

This positive experience of the cognitive dimension supports the claim that debating provides an ideal pedagogy for developing vocabulary (Aclan & Aziz, 2015), alongside a positive approach to challenging oneself to engage – as outlined by Curran (1972) – when Valentina says that she forces herself to speak.

On the whole, however, this process was reported by the participants in relation to the receptive skill of listening, thereby supporting Krashen's comprehensible input hypothesis whereby learners acquire new language only when their language level is adequate for the new grammar or vocabulary to be assimilated (Krashen & Terrell, 2000). Indeed, there is more recent and growing evidence that supports the power of metalinguistic knowledge to aid the development of EFL speaking (Ganem-Guitérrez & Nogués-Meléndez, 2013). However, the same essential process applies also to that of language output, whereby participants attempt to recall language and utilize it in speaking. This process has been conceived of as the comprehensible output hypothesis and argues that speaking and writing play a significant role in driving language acquisition (Swain & Lapkin, 1995). Generally, participants reported that they attended the debates more for comprehensible output than input. Indeed, the comprehensible input hypothesis is argued to be inadequate as a sole source of acquisition and that output is also required (Swain & Lappin, 1995; Whong, 2011). The motivation of the learners and their experience suggests that from this aspect of the cognitive experience, the debate group pedagogy fulfils all of the CELTA teaching qualification assessment criteria, from the initial course planning to its execution (Table 1).

The participant's conscious learning strategies of comprehensible input and comprehensible output can be considered as language learning strategies that play a role in language acquisition, as Whong (2011) concludes. Participants' notetaking during the debates can also be seen as evidence of the processes involved in input and output as language is identified and operated on. Again, what the application of these approaches demonstrates is an independent ability to self-direct learning thanks to prior experience of learning (Luria, 1994; Lantolf & Thorne, 2006). It is important to highlight the existence of these strategies as they represent a crucial role in the debate group as ELT pedagogy, as it suggests that the learners can independently structure their individual language learning. The only caveat here is that they have acquired an Elementary level of grammar and vocabulary that can be drawn on in order to debate; a skill that is possible at the Elementary level (Council of Europe, 2021).

In proposing debates as a form of ELT pedagogy, perhaps, such metacognitive strategies could be taught or recommended within a structured curriculum wherein learners research the topic and use their metacognitive abilities to reflect on the language related to the topic. Afterward, they could follow up by revising the language they will then use in the debate, making notes during the debates to further identify new language which can potentially be integrated into their linguistic repertoire.

The participants' abilities in perceiving these issues highlighted their ability to discover and monitor their metalinguistic cognitive strengths and weaknesses. It was reported by the majority of the group that the design of the debate sessions fosters this reflection, which suggests that the debate group provides good opportunities for the participants to monitor, notice and apparently learn or improve knowledge of grammar and vocabulary. As Whong (2011) and Lantolf and Thorne (2006) have observed, the monitoring of others' EFL errors and comparing them to one's own as means of 'Noticing' new language features are metacognitive tools that can have a considerable impact on converting Interlanguage into the target language. That the debate group contains such communication which can foster metacognitive reflection suggests that it is not only a conversation that is taking place, but rather, a pedagogy that continually feeds and supports acquisition through reading during their debate-topic research, listening during the debates, and writing during their research and during the debates. These affordances suggest that it is a humanistic form of pedagogy, as participants are receiving an education that fulfils their objectives to either maintain or improve their cognitive-linguistic capacity and other related learning goals. As Larsen-Freeman observes (2011), there are many ELT methods that are not structured in such a way and that do not challenge learners so that their language resources are drawn on to the same degree. Indeed, debating also fulfils the CELTA teacher assessment by employing an approach that connects diverse language skills (Cambridge English, 2021). This aspect of cognition intersects with the educational experience reported, insofar as the topics drawn from the participant's 'Thematic Universe' are more taxing than the often more simplistic, less demanding tasks described in one-to-one lessons (Salvatore, first interview) or conversation classes (Maria Grazia, first interview). These alternative forms of EFL were considered to be based on the sharing of more personal information in short-term disposable activities, and not on more complex in-depth discussion of discourses that connect personal experience to history or society at large; that is, in addition to the multiple language skills that the pedagogy demands.

As Curran's process of experience shows, my role as 'the other' has a direct impact on every aspect of the experience including the cognitive. However, it is only through enquiry into the experience of cognition that light can be shed on my role. As I have argued by adopting Curran's model, cognitive development can be nurtured by promoting an overall positive learning experience, which involves the ways in which all of the themes relate to each other during a debate (Curran, 1972).

The social experience

Introduction

As previously stated, the social experience could be the one most immediately associated with the key concept throughout this book of humanism and education. The specific role that it plays and how it interacts with the other themes, however, is an issue that only a limited amount of research has drawn attention to (Norton, 2013). This theme suggested that there was a 'softer' aspect to the participants' attendance, insofar as it was not a purely intellectual pursuit. During the first two years, this was not obvious to me, and yet it is clear from the interviews that they partook in the debate group as a way of socializing. The participants remarked on how their relationships within the debate group were based on social cohesion, where there was mutual respect for each other's views, even when they might diverge. This should not be surprising given the research evidence within adult education that has demonstrated the fundamental importance of developing social skills (OECD, 2015).

> I think that it is important for confrontation and relationships, I think it's important in our life to have relationships. (Maria-Grazia, first interview)

> I find myself in a good way in this group – comfortable – because there are good relations among everyone … for me it is a comfortable moment when I come here for the debate. I feel first class (laughs) sorry, but it's my state of feeling, psychologically. (Laura, first Interview)

As indicated throughout the themes of communication, education and cognition – the social dynamics, which in psychology are referred to as Group Dynamics have been long understood as fundamental to understanding both the positive and negative experiences of a social group (Forsyth, 2006). However, such insights from psychology have not been applied in second language acquisition studies (Dornyei & Ryan, 2015). The reason why group dynamics is of such importance as far as the debate group goes is that – as highlighted earlier on in the book – speaking is by far the most challenging skill for language learners (Thiriau et al., 2017). It stands to reason, therefore, that insights from the psychology of the group could inform pedagogy and curriculum planning.

A socially-determined curriculum and pedagogy

Though there are no doubt differing degrees of the ratio between cognitive demand and positive affect (i.e. talking with friends about last night's television vs a chess club meeting), the social experience of the group was not viewed as a chance collateral by-product of the aim to debate, but rather an integral part of it. This highlights an area of relative neglect in ELT research where students' experiences may often be taken for granted or not explored (Dufva, 2013). Where previous studies have been undertaken, the social context has been found to be of great significance (Norton, 2013). The concern is that this under-specification can lead to a 'natural' social distance between teacher and student, unchallenged due to local cultural practices, and create an uncomfortable gap between students, again, depending on the lottery of personality and local cultural differences that many an EFL teacher finds themselves in.

The significance and relevance to the present study of Curran and Freire's work as humanistic educators is that they assume that the starting point of curriculum design and pedagogy is in how people interact with one another and thus in the social context and environment fostered by the teacher (Curran, 1972; Freire, 1972, 1974). It is based on an understanding of the human, of differentiating, not only in a strictly cognitive manner regarding language level but by trying to accommodate each personality and their higher needs. The teacher is responsible for the orchestration of this to begin with, as they set the aims and communicative dynamics of the debate. However, as the debate group demonstrated, this is an ongoing and evolving process that evolved between the first and last interviews. Indeed, the interviews became a part of the debate pedagogy as they involved the teacher seeking feedback from the students and adapting the pedagogy to meet their educative-emotional needs, with a view that this could significantly determine the potential level of their language learning and the degree to which they participate. Within this context, there appears to be no separation between communication, education or cognition from the social experiences of such a form of language pedagogy. This reflects what Curran refers to as education being a 'total-person process'; 'contrasted with this conception is a highly intellectualized idea of learning as separate from the other complex and subtle psychosomatic processes in the human personality' (Curran, 1972, 19). The socially-determined curriculum and pedagogy are therefore contrasted.

> ... an abstractly intellectual or conditioning one; rather the learning process is viewed as an expression of a unified psyche-soma. The process involves abstraction and conditioning, but also includes the spontaneity of instincts and emotions, especially those of defence and anxiety. These psychosomatic aspects of humankind combine with concrete and abstract learning functions as well as voluntary motivation.
>
> (Curran, 1972, 20)

The clear benefits of this are that all aspects of an individual's experience are taken into account so as not to neglect aspects of the experience that could lead to a lack of unity, thus rendering an aspect of, and therefore the overall experience, a potentially less positive experience for the learner.

A community of interest

> It's my pleasure to come here and hear what my companions say. (Valentina, first interview)

The social experience of debating transpired to be a bona fide community that drove an educational process that participants created and shaped week by week. Through communicating 'hearing what my companions say' about a topic that they are interested in that is derived from their Thematic Universe. Debating created a Community of Interest held together by a shared set of concerns and motivations, centred on the act of debating. Each member shared the same concern to communicate via dialogue and debate as a means of making sense of their past and present life experiences, with a frequent view to the future. Each member of the community had in common the same life stage; that of post-retirement, with the desire to utilize their intellect in a communicative context, with others of a similar culture. No single member could resolve this concern alone, but rather needed the community to manifest this activity; as if the debate group was a way of resuscitating aspects of the social world that they had once partaken in, but at this point in their lives they had grown out of. In feeling their loss, they sought a form of social communication that would resolve it.

That this social-communal aspect of the participant's experience emerged as significant in the debating as a humanistic form of pedagogy is evident in the data where peer-learning and dialogic communication were so central, highlighting the importance of a 'total-person process' or 'whole-person' model (Curran, 1972) to education; all aspects of the experience of the debate group related to each other. In this sense:

> The word 'community', therefore, is intended to envelop a living task-orientated experience between teacher-knower and learner-student, and not simply to suggest a group as such. The term is intended to introduce, in addition, the intense self-involved and self-committed dynamics that common group commitment would imply.
>
> (Curran, 1972, 30)

A humanistic pedagogy is conceived of therefore more as a homogeneous community, not from the perspective of cognitive abilities of language levels only, as is more often the case when grouping together students (Larsen-Freeman & Anderson, 2011), but rather from the perspective of the participants and the teacher as social beings in communion. Some of the data did relate the challenges to the aspect of the debate group that does not manage differentiation very well, as previously discussed in relation to cognitive language ability, and this represented the only real weakness of the pedagogy and was the main threat to it being less humanistic. This suggests that the cognitive experience does play a part in creating a humanistic pedagogy, but that it only compromises the fifth-level learners who take displeasure in listening to what they perceive sometimes as being participants who struggle to express themselves. Nonetheless, these same individuals overwhelmingly value much of the communicative, educational, cognitive and affective aspects of their experience. Additionally, the debate group still offers a method of language education that is more appropriate for the participants concerned than the other forms that they have compared the debate group to.

Another point of interest regarding the social experience is its under-specification in teacher assessment (Table 1) which generally favours more specifically cognitive language teaching-learning goals. This is the first and clearest example of how the standardized teacher assessment criteria appear to be lacking what is otherwise an important aspect of the wider educational experience according to learners; the social. It is interesting that the recent emphasis on social and emotional learning and social and emotional skills in education and employment (OECD, 2015, 2019, 2021) is relatively limited in contemporary language teacher training at the entry-level 1; (Cambridge English, 2021). In the following section, we will see how the criteria are also limited from the second type of affective experience, currently conceived outside of language teaching as emotional learning or skills (OECD, 2021).

What is particularly interesting, when taking into consideration the accounts of the social experience, is how participants can be seen to reflect the ascent through the various stages of Maslow's hierarchy of needs and have reached the final stage where they partake in the debate group as a way pursuing the final stage of self-actualization, along with those of Ego and Social Needs (Maslow, 1999). I would therefore argue that the examples of personal growth in relation to the other themes, though not as clearly stated, are also further evidence that participants are not motivated by an instrumental need that corresponds to lower needs such as Safety and Physiological Needs. This would suggest that the debate pedagogy is humanistic for them and that they have a very acute awareness of the positive role that it plays in their lives. Both Freire (1974) and Curran (1972) maintain that language education is an arena in which such affective goals can be fulfilled. What Maslow's theory (1999) captures however is a broader perspective of the language learner beyond the classroom, and how EFL education does indeed have the potential to be a way of achieving humanistic goals that go beyond the narrower vision of some methods, and beyond the explicit content of many language schools' mission statements (Curran, 1972; Larsen-Freeman & Anderson, 2011).

The role of the teacher-knower as counsellor

It was only through reflecting on the interviews that they seemed to have played the role of counselling sessions whereby each participant, had the chance to share their experience with the teacher. I saw it therefore as my responsibility when facing the participants to follow up on what they had shared with me, and through my managing of the group dynamics try to ensure that their concerns were dealt with as far as possible. At every point, this was done to fulfil the humanistic needs of the participants from the methodological perspective yet was also unexpected and seemingly inseparable from the debate group pedagogy as a whole. As Alexander (2020) attests:

> If students need to talk (dialogue) in order to learn about the world, teachers need to talk in order to learn about students.

In addition, it is also related to the communicative-educational dimension. Clearly, this reflects a concern for the curriculum (education) and pedagogy (communication) with the specific aim in mind that the two – when appropriate – result in personal transformation, or 'becoming' as Curran (1972) refers to it. Becoming could be in part at least interpreted as relating to the general sense of enjoyment and well-being that I witnessed and that participants generally expressed. This is a role that Curran charges the teacher with; to foster this distinctive rapport with the learner, which could be taken for granted or ignored (Curran, 1972). In Curran's teaching method, this is referred to as the 'Reflection Phase' and takes place at the end of the lesson. By the teacher-knower offering this opportunity for feedback, he or she is becoming 'Incarnate' as he or she takes a risk of being criticized. The counsellor-teacher-knower thus relinquishes the 'God-project' of being in control and invulnerable, in favour of promoting the learners' sense of personal growth termed by Curran as 'Redemption' and 'Congruence' (Curran, 1972). This rapport that was fostered between the teacher-knower as 'other' is said to promote the second conceptualization of 'Redemption', in Curran's theory of the learner in becoming the incarnate 'I-myself'. This leads to the formation of the 'I-myself-other' relationship which promotes Redemption, as the individual is unified within and externally with the teacher. In this sense, the learner has resolved the conflict inherent in becoming a successful language learner between the 'I' and the 'myself', and additionally resolves the conflict posed by the teacher. The one-to-one session, therefore, could potentially provide the learner with 'a feeling of self-worth and value which a growing sense of unique self-acceptance produces' (Curran, 1968 in Stevick, 1990, 81). This aspect of the counselling-learning approach as a humanistic method involves 'the teacher voluntarily giving up some of the safeguarding that is provided by most other teaching styles' (Stevick, 1990, 94) which does not factor in this stage; due to the teacher's opening themselves up to receiving feedback on their teaching.

Though not as specific as the outline of affective experience that I have described so far, there is some consideration of such student consultation in all of the CELTA teacher assessment criteria (Table 1). Insofar as the teacher is responsible for 'teaching according to the needs of learners' (Cambridge English, 2021), there is the implication that this teacher knowledge derives from enquiring to some degree and in some manner what the learner's learning objectives are with respect to curriculum and pedagogy. My role which emerged as a result of interviewing reflects this. From this perspective, the teaching criteria ensure a degree of concern for positive affect. The extent to which this can be evidenced in relation to promoting the attainment of higher needs is less explicit, however, and is presumably taken to be a by-product of meeting the criteria. While I believe that the debate group pedagogy suggests that raising awareness of the importance of the social and affective dimensions is vital, in line with current research mentioned so far (Dewaele et al., 2019; OECD, 2021), the CELTA criterion in my view implies this outcome as a result of meeting the criteria to a sufficient level. In sum, all of the CELTA criteria – according to participants – are met to some degree.

On the whole, each of the experiences described by participants, I would argue demonstrate that while the social may be the most obvious of humanistic considerations in education, its role is one that impact and depends on that of communication, education, and cognition. To reiterate, it is only through taking a humanistic stance and applying it to educational enquiry that these relationships emerge that emphasize the experiential nature of language teaching and learning (Curran, 1972; Norton, 2013; Dewaele et al., 2019).

Debating as holistic education

The following section will distil the two most arguably significant outcomes of the discussion into two parts, as an introduction to the following penultimate chapter which provides a possible way of integrating the kind of non-competitive, didactic, dialectical and dialogic debating that has been presented so far – within a pedagogy and curriculum. The two outcomes include the way in which the four categories are experienced alongside the dual process of the five stages of acquisition and personal growth.

The five dimensions as holistic

Firstly, debating has been conceived as a form of potentially holistic education that comprises the educational, communicative, cognitive and social dimensions. In a sense, though each is dynamic and comes to life in new ways in each debate, potentially: the dimensions represent categories, albeit categories that enter into a kind of process as they fluidly emerge and interact as natural parts of dialogic speaking and a subjective and objective curriculum. While the categories that have emerged are somewhat predictable, their significance lies in the argument that this lens is one that is seldom reflected in SLA research. Furthermore, that this framework could support teachers in their pedagogical and curriculum planning as a way of approaching their contexts and therefore as a first step in diagnosing a new class or cohort, i.e. while teachers no doubt often subconsciously plan to some degree using some of the themes highlighted that they could benefit more consistently from the application of such a framework.

Likewise, teacher trainers and indeed researchers may gain more of a multi-dimensional, holistic understanding of SLA were they to include these categories in their regular planning.

The five stages as developmental process (acquisition and redemption)

The second part is that of the personal process that Curran represents as a series of stages through which the learner can choose through engaging in the debates and respecting his or her fellow participants through listening and learning (Figure 2).

The five stages that have been discussed in the previous chapter present a clear process of simultaneous language acquisition with a theory of personal growth. This theoretical correspondence that the research is only suggestive of – given that an actual analysis of objective acquisition was not undertaken due to the focus on the experiential dimension of the research – nonetheless – has gained weight in psychology. McAdams's research in the first part of the twenty-first century has utilized the term 'Redemptive-self' (McAdams & Adler, 2006; McAdams, 2001) to describe a very similar psychological process as the one which Curran described some forty-odd years prior in his presentation of the counselling-learning approach (Curran, 1972). Indeed, in Dornyei and Ryan's rare state-of-the-art review, they argue that this concept of McAdams corresponds to a larger theory of the role of personal narrative in second language learning and that this forms one of the most recent developments in the psychology of SLA. Dornyei and Ryan also point out the importance of contextualizing such studies within the applied discipline that the psychology of the language learner involves, including in the formal educational contexts which learners inhabit (2015).

Though Dornyei's model is of interest as it appears to complement the possible stages that the learner can go through, with respect to the debate group its focus on motivation is not as immediately relevant. The relevance on the other hand of Curran's approach as a psychological approach to the language learner, which Dornyei argues for (2018), focuses on the L2 learning experience and highlights its complexity. It is useful as it reflects broader learning theories such as Vygotsky's well-known concept of the relationship of the internal and external plains (Lantolf & Thorn, 2006). The theory sees the learner's inner self as growing as a result of engagement with the social and the culture which is external. This reflexive dynamic reflects a product of genuine growth that captures the four categories, as each is experienced subjectively, often emotionally via affective experience or through *perezhivanie*. As Dornyei also argued, language teaching and education more generally have not been very quick to take on the insights from psychological research into group dynamics (2018). Dornyei's own approach is based on the prior stage to the student's participation in this educational process which begins at the motivational stage. Indeed, his proposal for a motivational-self system is mediated by the psychology of an ideal L2 self which might be thought of as Curran's independent stage, with the 'Ought to self' which might be thought of as Curran's I-myself, and the actual L2 learning experience as the contextual aspect which arguably comprises the main four themes which were identified in the debate group (communicative, educational, cognitive and social). I would suggest that these more recent theories build support for Curran's earlier innovative system and the importance of such approaches in the psychology of second language acquisition, as a way of increasing engagement in speaking tasks and activities.

Chapter conclusion

The following chapter provides what was found to be one way of supporting the outlined process discussed above. Of course, while this method can be reconstructed as a more general approach for the individual practitioner to reflect and work with, its motivation as a specific pedagogy and curriculum is to meet the needs of many teachers who call for such materials (Swan, 2012). Clearly, the methodologies of SLA researchers permeate the caution on their part not to prescribe specific methods, and this is widely accepted to be a sound approach, in an era where positivism has been found wanting in socially orientated research and education. Nonetheless, those scholars working closely with language teaching recognize the practical needs to train teachers and to provide ongoing support and updated training so as to inform their practice with research findings. This support which in some cases calls for prescription has the needs of the inexperienced teacher and their students at heart (Swan, 2012). It is with this in mind that the following chapter is presented to researchers, but more particularly to teachers at the chalk face who might be overwhelmed by planning their early years of teaching, which can present a great challenge (Swan, 2012).

In sum, the 'theme and process' approach developed through the research seeks to suggest that while indeed complex in comparison with some of the more standard grammar-translation methods, or the more superficial isolated speaking activities that debating offers the basis of pedagogy and curriculum that is able to meet the needs of teachers and learners in developing speaking. As has been shown in this book, participants in the debate group required a safe speaking environment in which they could participate comfortably. The following quote provides a comprehensive summary of what up-to-date research on speaking in a foreign language has found, and is worth citing in full:

> Creating such a (safe and successful) speaking environment for speaking … appears to be a rather complex task, requiring constant juggling of multiple elements, including time, tasks, topics, peer relationships and feedback. In many ways, however, the task is also a most joyful one, for it goes far beyond creating conditions for a mere exchange of information in order to rehearse specific language features. Creating a safe speaking environment allows teachers to forge spaces – no matter how limited these may be within the countless constraints that most language educators face – which open up opportunities for students to lose themselves in the conversations that matter to them and that are consequential to their relationships with others and with the world around them. It takes time, endless patience and careful observation to transform possibilities that classroom talk offers into the actual benefits for students' language learning. But just like with speaking, this, too, is time well spent.
>
> (Kubanyiova, 2018)

This – I feel – describes my own conclusion which I experienced in my role as a practitioner-researcher. I was involved with the participants before, during and after the research, reflecting and reading in an effort to understand better how debating as a means of teaching speaking can be improved, and complement a broader curriculum so that both teachers and students benefit from an enhanced and deeper approach to the most important skill by far that learners are faced with teaching (Kubanyiova, 2018). I would only add that a consultative or collaborative approach to debating as a form of classroom communication be also key for many learners – as in comparison with a competitive one – as it may increase the creation of a safe learning environment that both teachers and learners perceive as being the key foundation for improving their acquisition and experience of it.

9

An Integrated Curriculum and Pedagogy for Debating

Introduction

The following section provides a step-by-step guide for the English language teaching practitioner and course designer that can be employed to plan an entire school or academic year. Based on the research cited so far in this book, the proposed pedagogy and curriculum should be adaptable for a large number of learners in a variety of contexts. The following method can be thought of as a form of TBL that also potentially accommodates aspects of the lexical approach. It may be particularly useful for developing from the intermediate level upwards, in the following contexts:

- Middle school ESL & EFL English
- High school ESL & EFL English
- University ESL & EFL English
- Adult ESL & EFL

What follows is a convenient exposition that reflects a format that will probably be familiar to many teachers who employ textbooks. Indeed, the reader will find a specific cycle of lesson plans provided to make clearer how the general curriculum template could be applied to a single cycle of lessons (four one-hour lessons approximately). This is aimed to support the teacher in their practice so that they are able to easily adapt to suit their student's interests or needs. The difference in the sample unit here, however, is that it offers a template for successive units, each unit potentially providing as many as four lessons, though potentially more. A topic and accompanying text contained in the example unit serve as an example of how an article can be drawn on as the centrepiece of a series of lessons, instead of being used as a one-off reading activity that may last one hour at the most. The idea is to make the most of such a text and place a responsibility on both the teacher and the student to give and take more from the text, engaging in a dialogue with it, so that deep learning can take place.

The basic pattern for each unit which corresponds to a particular topic begins and ends with a speaking and listening task. While often student dialogue is considered to be a speaking task, in reality, it involves learners speaking to each other, and therefore listening also; this, in fact, reflects the kind of debate that has been presented and is being proposed. Furthermore, it is a dialogue that is valued, as it initiates the unit and sets the boundaries for the contextualization of the reading as input which is often introduced as THE text, instead of a text just like that of the student's opinion or experience of the topic. The written text which is to be read should probably be discursive, inviting learners to discuss and argue over issues that it raises, so it can be challenged or added to by the learner who is invited to speak about the topic as presented in the reading before the reading even takes place. The text should not be taken as a fact to be learned, but rather as a source of stimulation for learners. The learners as speakers then comment on the text, asserting, and balancing their views and experiences; the written text does not have the final word. If there are any new language points that arise, this is an opportunity for the learner to learn new language with other students and the teacher, as the new language is absorbed by the learner, empowering their expressive powers. The learner notes down – according to a shared understanding – the meaning and contexts of the new language. The learners are guided by the book and the teacher to draw on their speaking, listening, and new language to formulate a statement and a contribution to the topic that is theirs. Once the learner has completed this, they then present their position with clarity to their group, thus contributing to a shared knowledge building.

Each unit assures the student that their voice and the voices of their fellows provide the starting and finishing word before moving on to the next unit which reemploys the same stages. This predictability provides learners with a clear set of expectations from themselves, their peers, and the teacher. It provides a framework for learning all four language skills, in addition to more general knowledge, applied to meaningful spoken and written texts that promote the learner to reflect and engage as a member of their class, and a way of communicating in society at large.

Context and rationale

At middle school age, learners are beginning to reason in a new manner as their abstract reasoning develops and they engage with others in new ways more discursive ways. While it may not yet be common practice in some contexts, teachers are encouraged to introduce learners to the model, so that as they transition through each year of middle school, and then to high school. In this way, they are more likely to be expected to take responsibility for their learning in the way that it is conceived herein, i.e. that they begin something which they are given the chance to finish: by providing learners with a task to be completed by the end of a lesson that provides them with a result, and that connects to the following lesson or lessons, but without giving them a sense of incompletion. This could also increase engagement and therefore reduce disruption or lack of concentration. The model provides both the teacher and learners with a structured four-stage pedagogy that is flexible enough to be managed according to time constraints, holidays, school closures, exams etc. All that is required is that the teacher, and indeed the learners, be permitted to employ and partake in what may be considered a novel approach.

A standard unit

Lesson 1

Rationale and aim

The aim of the lesson is to introduce students to a new topic, a target written text to read, and to discuss it with each other. By the end of the lesson, the students will have read all of a text and will have shared their opinions and experiences on the topic by the end, and have begun to highlight any new language.

Procedure

1. In the first lesson, the teacher introduces a topic and an opening question to be discussed.

The discussion can be done in groups of a minimum of two to probably around five students. In this way, learners draw on their opinions and experiences in relation to the topic, so that they are immediately engaging in listening and speaking to each other.

Table 3 The continuity of the lesson debate course cycle

Lesson 1	Lesson 2	Lesson 3	Lesson 4
Speaking & Reading Comprehension	Reading & Language study (of text from lesson 1)	Writing (of text type that was read in lesson 1)	Speaking (Debate)

2. A written text is presented by the teacher, ideally to each individual, which could be in the form of any number of texts that the teacher is interested in the students' learning.

Examples of developing both reading and writing could be an article, an essay, a letter/email, a review, a short story, a proposal and a report. The aim is for the students to be introduced to a written way in which they can structure a way of expressing something about the topic, regardless of the text type, i.e. students could write a letter about a holiday or read an article about it. The text provides the students in their groups a way of deepening their knowledge of the topic itself and/or the target language which learners are trying to learn as language learners.

3. The teacher provides the students with a further question to discuss related to the new information provided in the text.
4. The final phase of the lesson is the answering of a set of comprehension questions on the text that also serve as the source of new language points to be discussed in the second lesson. The teacher should aim to provide the answers to the questions by the end.

Lesson 2

Rationale and aim

While students may have already asked some questions about new vocabulary in lesson 1, this second lesson is the first which is dedicated to the explicit study of vocabulary, grammar, collocations, or even pronunciation. As there is often a demand from stakeholders to teach explicit grammar, this could be the first point at which to introduce some grammar exercises that relate to the specific grammar, e.g. in the reading of a short story, some exercises on narrative exercises could be completed, as they will be employed by students during their writing in lesson 3, and also to some extent during the debate in lesson 4. Some teachers might like to use a specific grammar book, printed exercises, online exercises etc. By the end of the lesson, learners will have begun to study grammar, vocabulary, and collocations contained within the text and any other language that they might need to translate. All of the exercises provided should be completed.

Procedure

1. Remind students of the previous lesson where the text was introduced, and draw their attention back to it. Pre-teach, briefly any language items that might be new, then invite students to ask questions about any new language items.

2. Hand out the exercises and ask students to re-read alone, ask if there are any new language items again.
3. Ask students to complete the exercises alone or in groups of two or small groups.
4. Monitor pairs, supporting them where needed. Note any newly emerging items and potentially review them with the class once the exercises have been completed.
5. Inform learners that in the following lesson, they will write their version of the text.

Lesson 3

Rationale and aim

In the previous two lessons, the learners engaged with the written text and familiarized themselves with the topic and the associated language. In this lesson, some analysis of the structure of the text will take place and will be guided by the handout which highlights the overall structure and associated language. The students should write the whole of the text during class, receiving support from the teacher where necessary. This piece of writing will be an opportunity for the learners to begin to consider and formulate their position on the topic as a segue to the following final lesson in which they will discuss their views on the topic. It is recommended that teachers familiarize themselves with the content and process of the text, and follow a basic guide of how to do this. While a single lesson is indeed a short amount of time to introduce how to write a text and to write it, the curriculum is designed to ensure that the learners will receive evenly repeated opportunities to write the same genres, the teacher choosing which ones to provide formative or summative assessments for. A genre approach to analysing the features of the written text according to their language function, from the macro level of paragraph to the micro level of vocabulary and grammar is recommended.

Procedure

1. Remind the students that they will be writing their version of the text which they have read.
2. Draw on the board, or project the text so that all learners can see it. Highlight the basic structure which should reflect the labelling of the function of each paragraph that is highlighted in the handout, along with some of the key language features such as tense, frequency of adverbs/adjectives, distribution of pronouns as indicated for the specific text as indicated in the writing guide.

3. Ask students to begin to write, monitoring and supporting where necessary.
4. Collect writing at the end of the lesson, reminding learners that they will revisit the writing of the target text on numerous occasions, ideally at specific points that the teacher can plan from the beginning of the year and be sure to mark according to the criteria provided in the writing guide.
5. Remind students that in the next lesson, they will be partaking in a debate. Provide them with the specific question, and provide either paper or online resources to deepen their knowledge on the topic. This stage can also be considered to offer a further opportunity to read. The content of the further reading may offer an opportunity for extended language learning, though this is not the main objective. Rather, it should be considered to be an opportunity for those who wish to learn more about the topic. For those who for whatever reason do not choose to research further, they can draw on their own experiences, views, those of others and those from the article.

Lesson 4

Rationale and aim

Even if the key text was an email to a friend which is not a debating/argumentative text, the topic of the text can be reformulated into a debate question. For example, if the learners are asked to write an email to a friend who has asked for advice on whether he or she should go on holiday with their parents, the debate question for young people could be whether they think young people should go on holiday with their parents. This can be tweaked according to the issues and concerns that the teacher is aware of that affect the students. The idea is that learners have the opportunity to share their thoughts, verbally with the members of their debating group, so that two forms of output (writing and speaking) are employed in quick succession from one lesson to the next. This lesson will bring the unit to a close, before the four-lesson cycle restarts.

The debate questions could relate to the main written text and reading and include the following or variations thereof;

1. Should the government provide free healthcare for all citizens?
2. Is social media more beneficial or harmful to society?
3. Should the legal drinking age be lowered or raised?
4. Is it better to rent or buy a house?
5. Should the death penalty be abolished?

6. Is it more important to focus on economic growth or environmental protection?
7. Should genetically modified foods be allowed?
8. Is it acceptable to use animals for scientific experiments?
9. Should the voting age be lowered to 16?
10. Is it better to work for a large corporation or start your own business?
11. Should all countries have open borders?
12. Is homeschooling a better option than traditional schooling?
13. Should the government regulate the use of artificial intelligence?
14. Is it ethical to use animals for entertainment, such as circuses or zoos?
15. Should recreational drug use be legalized?
16. Is it better to pursue a university education or learn a trade?
17. Should the government provide subsidies for renewable energy sources?
18. Is it fair for athletes to be paid such high salaries?
19. Should smoking be banned in all public places?
20. Is it important to preserve traditional cultural practices?

These questions cover a range of topics and can generate interesting discussions among adult ESL learners. Remember to encourage learners to express their opinions and provide supporting arguments during the debates.

Procedure

As the students debate, the teacher can remind learners of these principles and procedures of etiquette etc. The basic findings and procedure are to encourage the quieter members to share more often, and for the more vocal among them, to listen more, so that each member of the debate groups has a more equal possibility of expressing themselves, listening to other's ideas, and ultimately learning about others experiences and others' perspectives.

If the teacher wishes to hold a whole class debate, then the teacher would play the role of the chair. In smaller groups, the teacher could move around the groups chairing where necessary. The teacher may remind learners about the group dynamics proposed by Curran (1972), so that quieter learners push themselves more to contribute, and more talkative learners give space and encouragement to quieter participants to speak.

1. Debate topic posed at the end of the debate.
2. Participants research the topic and, prepare thesis.
3. Debate question is provided at the start of the debate so as to remind participants.

4. Each participant is given up to five minutes to deliver their thesis.
5. Participants engage in freer debate, chaired by teacher-chair who occasionally supports the discussion or assists with language items.
6. At the end of the debate the new debate topic is provided, and the cycle goes on.

Post overview and rationale of lessons and unit

The above table (Table 3) tracks the basic development of four lessons in which students deal meaningfully with a single text drawing on all language skills (reading, writing, speaking and listening), therefore providing a more student-centred focus on output and potential for individual engagement, focus on the language itself, in the form of naturally occurring grammar and vocabulary, with attention to collocations. In some schools, this might amount to two weeks of class time, in others perhaps one week. This is not important, however. What is key is that the topic is developed over time, though each stage has a clear goal that must be reached by the end of the lesson. The topic is developed in a dialogic manner that engages the learners based on their experience and knowledge and therefore gives each learner the opportunity to listen and learn from each other, whilst simultaneously having a piece of reading that they can refer to as a source of guidance and information that is perhaps more objectively focused, therefore creating a balance of knowledge types. The teacher has two clear occasions in which to focus on teaching language in the second lesson when the reading is analysed and at the writing stage when the teacher has the opportunity to grade and support the development of text structure, and language. In the fourth and final stage, the debates take place. The class could carry out the debate as one group, depending on the size of the class and the dynamics which are familiar to you as a teacher. Alternatively, a class of twenty-five students, for example, could be divided into as many as five small groups, or as few as two. Again, this depends on class dynamics and can be experimented with to find the most effective number. During this stage, the teacher can move around the class observing, without intrusion each group, and potentially use the occasion to grade speaking, as long as the students are fully aware that this is the case, as it could be that students are not used to being graded on their spoken language contributions in this manner.

At the end of the four-stage cycle, the teacher has produced an even balance of input and output across all four language skills. In this way, there are plenty of opportunities for authentic language use for the students, and likewise, many diverse ways in which the teacher can assess learner progress. It is suggested, however, that students complete at least one cycle before necessarily grading them so that they have the opportunity to become familiar with the structure and expectations of the cycle. Indeed, it is worth providing the structure of the cycle to students, and potentially to parents, if an electronic online system is available where such information can be shared. This would aid students, parents, teachers, and the teacher's line managers as to how and what they are teaching. Parents view the pedagogy and curriculum so as to support their children if required.

(Sample Lesson plans for the four-lesson cycle)

Lesson 1: Speaking and reading comprehension

Many of the most popular, cutting edge and forward-moving cities in the world are cities in which a wide variety of people live together, ever moving towards greater unity, more than ever in human history. While our age has seen many challenges due to this integration of cultures, ultimately these environments continue to be the most important cities on the earth that move humanity forwards. Through being cultural melting pots, diverse and brilliant new ideas, and practices are born.

1. Talk with a partner

In which city and country would you expect
- to eat interesting food?
- to visit for sunbathing?
- to go underwater snorkelling?
- to visit art galleries and museums?

2. Reading

Work in pairs. You will read an article about four multicultural cities. Before you read, what do you think about multicultural cities?

Tokyo, Japan – A melting pot of cultures

Tokyo, the bustling capital of Japan, stands as a shining example of multiculturalism. This vibrant city is a harmonious blend of tradition and modernity, attracting people from all walks of life. Its international population, diverse cuisine and vibrant festivals make it a true global city. From the historic temples of Asakusa to the futuristic streets of Shibuya, Tokyo offers a unique cultural experience that reflects the spirit of both old and new.

New York City, USA – The cultural kaleidoscope

New York City, often called the 'melting pot', is a cultural kaleidoscope that embodies the essence of multiculturalism. This dynamic metropolis embraces diversity and celebrates the contributions of various communities. From Little Italy to Chinatown, Harlem to Brooklyn, each neighbourhood has its own distinct flavour and heritage. The city's iconic landmarks, world-class museums and bustling street life create an unparalleled cultural mosaic that leaves a lasting impression on all who visit.

Melbourne, Australia – A tapestry of cultures

Nestled in the southeastern corner of Australia, Melbourne shines as a true tapestry of cultures. With a rich multicultural heritage, this vibrant city embraces its diverse population, offering a multitude of experiences for residents and visitors alike. From the vibrant street art of Fitzroy to the aromatic flavours of the Queen Victoria Market, Melbourne's diverse neighbourhoods and thriving arts scene showcase the vibrant fabric of cultures that call this city home.

Toronto, Canada – Where the world comes together

Toronto, the largest city in Canada, proudly wears its multicultural identity. With over 200 ethnic groups represented, this cosmopolitan hub is a haven for cultural exchange. From the colourful festivals like Caribana and Diwali to the bustling neighbourhoods of Chinatown and Little Italy, Toronto offers a glimpse into the traditions and customs of various communities. The city's inclusive spirit, diverse culinary scene and thriving arts make it a true melting pot where the world comes together.

3. Now choose which of the answers is correct

1. What are some common characteristics shared by Tokyo, New York City, Melbourne and Toronto?

2. How would you describe Tokyo's cultural experience?
3. What makes New York City a cultural kaleidoscope?
4. Which city is known for its vibrant street art and diverse neighbourhoods?
5. What festivals can you experience in Toronto that showcase different cultural traditions?
6. How does Melbourne embrace its multicultural heritage?
7. What are some iconic landmarks or neighbourhoods you can explore in New York City?
8. How would you describe the overall atmosphere or spirit of these multicultural cities?

Lesson 2: Reading and language study

1. Match the following collocations:

a) Embrace diversity
b) Celebrate traditions
c) Thrive artistically
d) Reflect the spirit

Associations: Cultural diversity, cultural heritage, artistic community, cultural essence

2. Fill in the blank with the appropriate collocation: 'Tokyo offers a _____ blend of tradition and modernity.'

Answer options: harmonious, seamless, balanced, dynamic

3. True or False: 'New York City is renowned for its culinary _____.'

Answer: False (Replace the blank with 'delights' or 'scene')

4. Choose the correct collocation to complete the sentence: 'Melbourne's neighbourhoods showcase the _____ fabric of cultures.'

Answer options: vibrant, diverse, intricate, rich

5. Fill in the blank with the appropriate collocation: 'Toronto is a city that _____ cultural exchange.'

Answer options: fosters, promotes, encourages, embraces
6. Match the following collocations:
   a) Dynamic metropolis
   b) Vibrant street life
   c) Unparalleled cultural
   d) Lasting impression

Associations: City, atmosphere, experience, impact
7. True or False: 'In Tokyo, you can find a harmonious _____ of old and new.'

Answer: True (Replace the blank with 'blend' or 'fusion')
8. Complete the sentence using the correct collocation: 'New York City's iconic landmarks _____ its vibrant culture.'

Answer options: embody, represent, symbolize, epitomize
9. Fill in the blank with the appropriate collocation: 'Melbourne's arts scene _____ with creativity and innovation.'

Answer options: thrives, flourishes, blooms, prospers
10. Match the following collocations:
   a) Embrace diversity
   b) Celebrate contributions
   c) Cultural mosaic
   d) Melting pot

Associations: Multiculturalism, various communities, diversity, cultural integration

Lesson 3: Writing

Write an article based on your visit to a city, town or village, following the instructions for article writing provided by your teacher. The below structure is provided below to support your writing. Notice the differences in parts of speech found in the Key grammar and vocabulary column. Consider why there are differences and similarities in between each stage. Try to use the example as a guide for your own writing.

(The teacher can lead the students in an analysis of each stage, exploring the various grammatical features and vocabulary to help students to learn how to write articles according to their specific features.)

Paragraph Stage	Key Grammar and Vocabulary
1) Introduction	Proper nouns, verb phrases, noun phrases
2) Festivals (sub-topic 1)	Adjective + noun phrases, nouns, verb + noun
3) Neighbourhoods (sub-topic 2)	Adjective + noun phrases, noun phrases, nouns
4) Inclusive Spirit (sub-topic 3)	Adjective + noun phrases, noun phrases
5) Conclusion	Noun phrases, adjective + noun phrases, nouns

Title: Toronto: A melting pot of cultures and diversity

1. Toronto, Canada's largest city, proudly showcases its multicultural identity. With representation from over 200 ethnic groups, it serves as a cosmopolitan hub, fostering cultural exchange and celebration. Festivals like Caribana and Diwali highlight the city's rich tapestry of traditions and customs. Toronto's inclusive spirit, diverse culinary scene, and thriving arts make it a true melting pot where the world comes together.

2. Toronto's multiculturalism shines through its vibrant festivals, such as Caribana and Diwali. Caribana, an annual Caribbean carnival, brings the city alive with music, colourful costumes, and energetic dances, offering a glimpse into the region's vibrant culture. Diwali, the Festival of Lights, illuminates Toronto's neighbourhoods as the Indian community comes together to celebrate with joy and grandeur.

3. The city's neighbourhoods further exemplify its multicultural essence. Chinatown and Little Italy buzz with activity, providing immersive experiences in Chinese and Italian cultures, respectively. Chinatown's lively streets offer authentic cuisine, herbal shops and a glimpse into Chinese customs. Meanwhile, Little Italy captivates visitors with its charming trattorias, gelato shops and vibrant festivals, celebrating the rich heritage of Italy.

4. Toronto's inclusive nature extends beyond its cultural festivities. Its diverse culinary scene offers a world of flavours, reflecting the city's multicultural fabric. From international cuisines in Kensington Market to local food festivals, Toronto invites residents and visitors to savour global tastes and appreciate the culinary contributions of different cultures. The city's thriving arts scene, encompassing museums, galleries, and theatres, serves as a platform for artists from diverse backgrounds to showcase their talents, promoting cross-cultural understanding and artistic exchange.

5. In conclusion, Toronto's multiculturalism is a source of pride and a testament to its identity as a melting pot of cultures. The city's festivals, neighbourhoods, culinary offerings and arts scene all contribute to an environment of inclusivity and cultural appreciation. Toronto truly embodies the spirit of unity, where people from around the world converge, celebrate diversity and create a vibrant tapestry of cultures in one dynamic city.

Lesson 4: Speaking (Debate)

1. Speaking (Debate)

In your group (teacher assigned) discuss what the pros and cons of living in a big city are, using the cities that you have read about and written about as a guide and to support your views.

2. Post-speaking

Write down the following:

Three new facts that you learned and why they were of interest to you

3. Speaking

Before you begin the next unit (Cycle 2) do some research into the topic 'independent investigation of truth' and some other key phrases such as 'religion and science'. Make some notes answering the following questions so that you can share with your partner or group your answers in a group discussion that your teacher will organize.

Conclusion

The research provides a clear actionable debate pedagogy that can extend to incorporating the main four key language skills. Where teachers have the freedom to design their own courses or augment them, the debate pedagogy outlined could be put to good use for potentially stimulating the development of the argumentative, discursive language associated with debating, and the wide array of topics, of interest to a given group of students. A clear four-lesson cycle has been provided that teachers can apply, as a way of increasing engagement through a potentially humanistic, dialogic form of speaking.

Implications for understanding adult speaking in TEFL

The research implies a number of ways in which the experiences of adult EFL speaking pedagogy in TEFL can be connected to current research into adult speaking in TEFL, and how these experiences can inform practical ways of delivering a novel approach to the teaching of speaking. However, its foundation is based on a humanistic stance regarding education throughout the study.

Teaching speaking in adult EFL involves consideration of at least four dimensions of the overall educational experience as outlined; Communicative, Cognitive, Educational and Social. The balance of these dimensions can be effected by both the teacher as a curriculum planner and selector of pedagogy/teaching method, and by participants, depending on broader situated educational objectives and characteristics of individual learners.

To develop EFL speaking, a diagnostic period in which the teacher gathers information about the objectives of the learners and the restrictions of the educational institution should occur at the beginning of a language course in which speaking is taught as a skill. In this manner, the likelihood of a curriculum and pedagogy that maximizes engagement and positive experience can be increased. During this stage, the emerging rationale for the pedagogy and curriculum, align with the four dimensions as a dynamic, interdependent set of factors. This could be achieved through the completion of a range of speaking tasks from language textbooks that are aligned to a broad yet specific level of English: the Cambridge range being one such example. Such tasks are designed to provide students with the opportunity to speak about a variety of topics that draw on a range of linguistic skills. Group speaking tasks with the teacher, smaller group tasks that the teacher monitors, and one-to-one groups that the teacher monitors and done as a group of three with the learners would provide a good overview of where to proceed in the design and use of other existing speaking tasks and activities.

Once the course commences there are two perceivable processes involved from the outset as indicated by the four-pointed star (Figure 1): From the participant's perspective, there are four dimensions that determine the affective quality of the other experiences; one enters the larger educational context and experiences on an affective scale, the communicative, educational, cognitive and social dimensions simultaneously. From the teacher's perspective, however – which involves pedagogical design and curriculum planning – the pedagogy is perhaps the primary determiner of affective experience in so far as participant's expectations are determined by the language skill being taught. A range of speaking tasks and activities can be tried, notes made on student performance, informal discussion about the student experience of the speaking tasks and activities, and student feedback forms provided. These combined methods could provide a useful overview on which to make decisions on continuous curriculum and pedagogical planning.

To ensure a positive communicative experience, the objectives of the learners with regard to their language skills and language knowledge should be sought by the teacher via group discussion, written feedback and informal chat. No doubt these specifics will vary from course to course and between learners. Communicative skills are often conflated with production via speaking and writing, however, comprehension via the receptive skills of listening and reading should also be considered at the stage of pedagogical planning. Furthermore, the way in which content knowledge of the language is communicated should also be taken into consideration. For example, while some learners may be keen to base their input on a coursebook or literary texts, others may prefer to learn a new language through conversation.

Regarding the educational dimension as conceived of as course content, the teacher and learners should be aware of the wider course content is determined by external curriculum planners within the institution. This can be done by consulting the educational policy of the school and consulting informally with colleagues. If there is a great degree of flexibility, then the onus is on the teacher to diagnose the needs of the learners. The teacher should continually gauge the impact and engagement of learner responses to the curriculum, and tailor it to the boundaries set by the institution and learners, in order to maximize positive experience of the wider educational experience.

There are two main sets of considerations regarding affect; one corresponds to the degree that the course, from the other dimensions, meets their expectations. For example, when the learner is motivated to practice speaking, the course provides the opportunity to actually practice speaking. The needs can be determined at the beginning of the course through questionnaires and direct discussion. The second is that of the higher affective dimension found in Maslow's hierarchy of needs which may be more elusive in defining at the outset of the course, but rather become more apparent after a rapport has been built up with the teacher, and then sought only when the teacher investigates via the kind of interviewing present in Curran's counselling-learning approach (1972) or in Freire's participatory action research (2008).

The social dimension can also be understood as being dependent on the other dimensions as an independent dimension. While the social dimension is necessary for fulfilling the expectations of developing, for example, the skill of speaking as it requires human contact, the extent to which an individual or a group of individuals happen to find a group of 'like-minded' fellow learners may increase or decrease the quality of their social experience. Indeed, in the debate group, this was also determined by the communicative dimension when fellow participants were perceived by the higher-ability speakers as possessing inadequate speaking skills to render the debates satisfying. It is worth, in such cases, consulting with management as to the possibility of moving students from one group to another early on in the course, or dividing the group into specific levels once their levels and communicative abilities have been established by the teacher. In some cases, the students may voice such concerns themselves thus aiding the teacher and the school.

While training to become a teacher is not exactly the same as training to become a psychologist, there is increasing awareness of the role that language educators play in the overall development of the learner, and sound calls have begun to emerge in ELT that call for ELT training to be informed by the body of research in psychology into issues such as 'group dynamics' that has so far not found their way into ELT discourse (Dornyei & Ryan, 2015; Dornyei, 2018; Dewaele et al., 2019).

Implications for understanding debating in adult TEFL

The research implies a number of ways in which the experiences of adult EFL debating as speaking pedagogy in TEFL can be connected to current research into adult speaking in TEFL, and how these experiences can inform practical ways of delivering a novel approach to the teaching of speaking. The emphasis however is based on the philosophical stance of humanism as an approach to educational enquiry.

A consideration of all four dimensions of experience suggests that debating has the potential to provide a holistic approach to adult EFL speaking as it draws on all four dimensions, engaging learners' educational, communicative, cognitive, affective and social skills.

As an educational experience, debating affords a Negotiated Syllabus in which learners collaborate with the teacher through a process of dialogic consultation. The curriculum is derived from the topics that interest the group instead of a non-negotiated grammar curriculum which is concerned with only the cognitive aspects of acquiring grammar and vocabulary (Larson-Freeman & Anderson, 2011). The content of the curriculum is supplied through the teacher observing the interests of participants as they emerge and is refined by the participants themselves through peer teaching-learning. The teacher facilitates this process and learns from the dynamics that peer learning and student-supplied content to inform future debate topics. This process has been described in the thesis and is evidenced in tabular format as a three-week cycle that can be indefinitely extended. Debating therefore can increase the enjoyment of the topics featured in an EFL pedagogy, as they are closely informed by the learners themselves.

The cognitive experience of debating as a pedagogy to use receptive and productive skills can be positive in its affordance to draw on metalinguistic knowledge, though stress or anxiety which creates pressure to speak can also be experienced negatively. This experience however is dependent upon how dialogue is managed by the teacher. The teacher should manage dialogue according to their ongoing evaluation of student speech and communicative relations, pre-empting difficulties where possible, and providing linguistic support in degrees via written and verbal feedback.

The social experience is defined by the group as a community of interest who congregate due to shared interests, and who are reliant on a community/group to instantiate the broader educational experience. As discussed, a positive group dynamic can be informally stimulated by giving the participants time in which to talk informally at the beginning and end of the class, uninterrupted in their first language, which often occurred in the debate group.

Debating can promote self-actualization; a higher form of affective experience due to the variety of challenges created by engaging in the communicative process as a speaker and/or listener, the educational experience as a teacher/learner as the learner teaches and learns, a cognitive experience that may foster the growth of language processing skills and increased knowledge of grammar and vocabulary via listening comprehension and speaking, and through the social experience as human contact and friendship can be fostered.

From the perspective of communicative experience, debating as a form of communicative dialogue has the potential to offer learners opportunities to practice both productive skills through speaking, and receptive skills of reading (during the research phase) followed by listening. An appropriate balance between production and reception can be created by working as a community to permit a positive affective learning experience, which is taken to be an important measure of the success of the pedagogy.

The three-stage pedagogy as has been outlined could be included in a teacher's English course or in a textbook. The three-stage pedagogy delivers a topic at the end of a debate so that participants can research it and formulate a thesis, thus promoting the skills of reading and writing in their note-making, followed by speaking about their thesis in the actual debate, then followed by additional reading in order to deepen their knowledge of the topic or new language in the week following the debate (see Table 3). In this way, a practical, actionable and novel debate model for EFL teachers is offered. The foundation of this approach is based on the humanistic stance of the research, in approaching educational planning.

Implications in relation to current debates about Artificial Intelligence and debating

In recent years the use of AI in language learning has arisen and been met with great enthusiasm, controversy and caution. Debating as a form of pedagogy perhaps reflects how both views associated with the technological turn can be approached at this time.

On the one hand, AI is able to comment on and assess language ability, comprising content and accuracy of grammar, vocabulary range, and pronunciation. Such feedback is possible without the presence of a human teacher and can provide quick and useful highlighting of errors and suggestions for improvement. From the philosophy of education approach and approach to SLA taken in this book, however, these aspects apply to declarative and technical knowledge of content and language and also to procedural knowledge found in performance; pronunciation being one clear example. What this book has argued for on the other hand is a human approach that begins with a teacher's efforts to understand the motivation of the students. Even if this motivation is technical, meaning based on declarative and procedural knowledge, the aims of the learner are to improve real communicational performance as reflected in real communicational contexts in social settings with other human interlocutors or audiences. Indeed, debating is strongly dialogical in character and therefore puts to the test the abilities and limits of AI. The key reason for this is that it is not yet entirely clear as to whether AI can offer a human language learner the often important affective component that a well-trained teacher with sufficient emotional intelligence can offer. This could perhaps be evidenced through psychological studies in which a language learner gauges the authenticity that a student feels AI could provide in chairing a debate. The AI would have to be able to discern and interpret individual personality, body language, individual history, engage in small talk in between lessons so as to get to know students and manage student interaction with great tact while continually gauging the complex nuances associated with human interaction; at least as far as contexts such as that highlighted in this single piece of research described. And while human teachers themselves may not be perfect in their abilities to give students what they need as the book has suggested, the question as to whether AI might be more able remains open at this time. It would indeed be a sophisticated technology that could potentially replace a teacher with the pedagogy discussed in this book.

All aspects of the affective or humanistic approach comprise a myriad of challenges for human teachers, and as the book has indicated, suggest that it is incumbent upon a teacher to listen, sympathize and empathize in a genuine manner that when successful is such that the student believes that the interlocutor shares their human experience. Again, the extent to which a language student would be motivated, assisted in their learning and satisfied with this experience if provided by a machine that by its own admission does not possess genuine subjective experience as it is not a living organic organism at this point in time is questionable.

Debating takes time and effort and is relatively costly in comparison with a language learning app or a would-be robot-debate chair. And yet, when considering the findings of the debate group and the affective experience of communication, education, cognition and social it is a sought-after pedagogy due to its affordances that according to learners offers a preferable way of learning a foreign or other language. Indeed, it could be surmised that in certain ways AI is a step backward towards the very traditional methods that treated language learning more as a logical exercise akin to mathematics than a dynamic process grounded in social context.

There is perhaps only one exception to how AI may indeed provide a useful debate chair or debating opponent, and that would be for students who are content to use AI as an interlocutor to 'spar' with. That is to say, the AI 'language teacher' satisfies a similar need to the chess player who is content to hone their chess skills with the kind of electronic chess sets which have been available since the 1980s.

Future research

There is still room for a much greater amount of research into employing debating as a method of teaching English as a foreign language. Given the ongoing growth of the TEFL sector and the primacy of the skill of speaking in adult TEFL, research into the issues highlighted could be useful for informing pedagogical design and curriculum development, to maximize holistic educational outcomes for students, teachers and schools. I would like to carry out further research into using debates in adult TEFL, perhaps in universities as there are a large number of adults in such contexts studying English as a foreign language. It could also be interesting to explore how the pedagogy would suit a business English context in which the broader skill of persuasive argument is employed. Researching other debate groups such as the one highlighted in other cities in Italy – although I am not currently aware of any – could also provide new insights. Issues related to the suitability of debating via online lessons could also be useful given the recent increase in online teaching. Ultimately, I would like to research and promote the humanistic dimension as one worthy of greater explicit attention, and to be combined as part of a broader holistic approach to both curriculum and pedagogical planning in TEFL.

Such research would support and build on the growing body of evidence that argues for the inclusion and consideration of social and emotional learning and skills in adult education to maximize the full range of educational outcomes in adult education through a holistic approach (OECD, 2015). The OECD's research findings and those of other independent researchers are gaining increasing momentum and are currently the focus of educators and schools within some national state educational contexts (Jones & Bouffard, 2012; Durlak et al., 2015; Brunskill, 2018). The global goal of promoting SES and SEL as an important dimension that must be included alongside other more traditional skill development in educational planning (National Scientific Council on the Developing Child, 2005/2014) supports Curran's research and counselling-learning theory (1972) as has been demonstrated in my research, the broad four experiences identified being in constant interplay and thus inseparable. This warrants more research into the experience of language skills and teaching in EFL in order to improve student and teacher outcomes (Dufva, 2013). More generally, as has been called for since the beginning of the communicative teaching period by both Horkheimer (1972) and Habermas (1974) in terms of the social sciences, and Jordan and Streets (1973) in school education, Curran (1972) and Freire (1972) in language teaching; aligning educational research and practice to its human base and away from the mechanized view of humankind could provide a more adequate whole understanding of the student and teacher. As has been argued throughout, the concerns of humanism when applied to education prioritize and can potentially elucidate many issues that occur within the educational context.

Final thoughts

Worldwide, the number of English as a foreign language learners is expected to continue to grow (British Council, 2021), though there exist varying motivations for individual learners and cultures (Lai, 2013; Setiyadi et al., 2019:). In Europe, TEFL takes place both in state schools (European Union, 2021) and in private language schools (British Council, 2021) in which the Common European Framework for Languages is adopted (Council of Europe, 2021). The focus on the eventual outcome of achieving a particular level of English as described by the CEFR is therefore widely taken to be the criteria by which a learner is successful. The overwhelming focus is on linguistic achievement captured by standardized testing. However, this emphasis on the cognitive does not incorporate the social and emotional skills that form a part of the overall language pedagogy and the experience of the language course from a social and emotional perspective. While large private English teaching chains for adults such as Wall Street English make mention of this dimension (Wall Street English, n.d.), they do so in a limited manner as reflected in the small amount of research into teaching speaking and affect evidenced in this thesis. This is significant for two reasons: firstly, some learners such as those found in the debate group are not motivated by the academic or career goals associated with much EFL in language schools, and therefore greater attention should necessarily be paid to developing the aspects of pedagogy and curriculum that are key to such learners. This could be seen as particularly pertinent to retired individuals who experience a gradual decline in self-esteem (Glassman & Hadad, 2013), and who therefore may benefit from such support, as found in studies with young adults more generally (OECD, 2015). Secondly, the affective experience is an essential dimension of the overall educational experience, the quality of which can determine the success of the learner, the student and, the educational institution. In sum, a broader holistic focus perhaps should not be taken for granted, as supported by the growing international research outside of the TEFL industry that emphasizes it as being fundamental to growth the and improvement of the individual and society (OECD, 2015, 2019, 2021).

As the debate group attested, all four dimensions combined and provided their impetus for participating every year. This contrasts with the short-term courses that reflect most English language student attendance in a language school as discussed. As Curran (1972) and Freire (1972: 1974) argued at the beginning of the communicative language period, the fundamental and basic recognition that humans, when engaged in education possess the potential to realize a unique set of transforming skills. I would suggest that it is due to the affordances of promoting higher-order needs, that participants are attracted to the combined curriculum and pedagogy of debating. For the attendees, there is no end to the course as they are able to continually, despite some communicative restrictions created by certain challenges of differentiation of language levels, nonetheless be challenged and challenge others by teaching and learning from peers.

Finally, while the framework of the discussion has been based on the four themes of cognition, communication and education, it is the experience of them that has been the focus of the thesis. Moreover, higher learning needs have been found to be the resulting maximal outcome for participants. Such an approach to education is clearly at odds with the other instrumental educational models in which a narrower, more materialistic motivation may guide the student in their path through EFL, and not consider what the student experience of this form of education actually is. With respect to my own practice, at least I as the practitioner-researcher can now apply what I have learned to help promote and maximize student experience when teaching EFL speaking so that this research can benefit learners.

Glossary

CHP	Cultural Historical Psychology
CHPT	Cultural Historical Psychological Theory
CHT	Cultural Historical Theory
CLL	Community Language Learning
CLT	Communicative Language Teaching
CRT	Critical Race Theory
EFL	English as a Foreign Language
ESL	English as a Second Language
EQ	Emotional Intelligence
L1	First Language
L2	Second Language
PP	Positive Psychology
SEL	Social and Emotional Learning
SES	Social and Emotional Skills
SLA	Second Language Acquisition
TEFL	Teaching English as a Foreign Language
TESOL	Teaching English to Speakers of Other Languages
TBL	Task-based Learning
TBLT	Task-based Learning & Teaching

Bibliography

Abdu'l-Bahá. (2011). *Paris Talks*. Wilmette, IL. Baháʼí Publishing.
Abdulmohsen Al Hassan, N. A. (2019). Saudi EFL University Instructors' Barriers to Teaching the Speaking Skills: Causes and Solutions. *Arab World English Journal*, 222, 1–53. DOI.org (Crossref), https://doi.org/10.24093/awej/th.222.
Aclan, E. M., & Aziz, N. H. A. (2015). Why and How EFL Students Learn Vocabulary in Parliamentary Debate Class. *Advances in Language and Literary Studies*, 6(1), 102–13. DOI.org (Crossref), https://doi.org/10.7575/aiac.alls.v.6n.1p.102.
Ahmed, A. S. (2018). The Debate in Islamic Tradition. *Oxford Research Encyclopedia of Religion*. DOI.org (Crossref), https://doi.org/10.1093/acrefore/9780199340378.013.475.
Ahmed, M. M. (2023). Oxford Reference. *Oxford Islamic Studies Online*. Retrieved from http://www.oxfordislamicstudies.com/article/opr/t236/e0534 (accessed 16 May 2023).
Akerman, R. and Neale, I. (2011). *Debating the Evidence: An International Review of Current Situation and Perceptions*. Research report, CfBT Education Trust. ISBN 978-1-907496-55-4.
Alasmari, A., & Salahuddin Ahmed, S. (2012). Using Debate in EFL Classes. *English Language Teaching*, 6(1), 147–52. DOI.org (Crossref), https://doi.org/10.5539/elt.v6n1p147.
Alexander, R. (2006). *Towards Dialogic Teaching: Rethinking Classroom Talk*. London. Dialogos.
Alexander, R. (2020). *A Dialogic Teaching Companion*. London. Routledge.
Al-Garni, S. A., & Almuhammadi, A. H. (2019). The Effect of Using Communicative Language Teaching Activities on EFL Students' Speaking Skills at the University of Jeddah. *English Language Teaching*, 12(6), 72. DOI.org (Crossref), https://doi.org/10.5539/elt.v12n6p72.
Al-Ghamdi, A. (2017). Building a Positive Environment in Classrooms through Feedback and Praise. *English Language Teaching*, 10(6), 37. DOI.org (Crossref), https://doi.org/10.5539/elt.v10n6p37.
Alikhani, M., & Bagheridoust, E. (2017). The Effect of Group Dynamics-Oriented Instruction on Developing Iranian EFL Learners' Speaking Ability and Willingness to Communicate. *English Language Teaching*, 10(11), 44. DOI.org (Crossref), https://doi.org/10.5539/elt.v10n11p44.
Al-Mahrooqi, R. I., & Tabakow, M. L. (2015). *Effectiveness of Debate in ESL/EFL – Context Courses in the Arabian Gulf: A Comparison of Two Recent Student-Centered Studies in Oman and in Dubai*, U.A.E. Second 21st Century Academic Forum Boston, USA at Harvard – 2015, 5(1) ISSN: 2330-1236.

Altun, M., & Ahmad, H. K. (2021). The Use of Technology in English Language Teaching: A Literature Review. *International Journal of Social Sciences & Educational Studies*, 8(1). Retrieved from https://www.researchgate.net/publication/354191052_The_Use_of_Technology_in_English_Language_Teaching_A_Literature_Review.

Anandari, C. L. (2015). Indonesian EFL Students' Anxiety in Speech Production: Possible Causes and Remedy. *TEFLIN Journal – A Publication on the Teaching and Learning of English*, 26(1), 1. DOI.org (Crossref), https://doi.org/10.15639/teflinjournal.v26i1/1-16.

Andrés, V. D., & Arnold, J. (2009). *Seeds of Confidence: Self-Esteem Activities for the EFL Classroom* (1st ed.). Helbling Languages.

Arabski, J., & Wojtaszek, A. (2010). *Neurolinguistic and Psycholinguistic Perspectives on SLA*. Multilingual Matters.

Aristotle. (n.d.). In *Encyclopædia Britannica*. Retrieved from https://www.britannica.com/biography/Aristotle (accessed 28 March 2023).

Aristotle. (2012). *The Art of Rhetoric*. London. Collins.

Arnaiz, P., & Pérez-Luzardo, J. (2014). Anxiety in Spanish EFL University Lessons: Causes, Responsibility Attribution and Coping. *Studia Anglica Posnaniensia*, 49(1), 57–76. DOI.org (Crossref), https://doi.org/10.2478/stap-2014-0003.

Arnold, J. (2011). Attention to Affect in Language Learning. Anglistik. *International Journal of English Studies*, 22(1), 11–22.

Asher, J. J. (2012). *Learning Another Language through Actions*. Sky Oaks Productions.

Assensoh, A. B. (1982). Debating and African Nationalism. *African Studies Review*, 25(1), 1–17. Retrieved from www.jstor.org/stable/523216.

Australian Institute of Aboriginal and Torres Strait Islander Studies. (2021). *Research Ethics Guidelines*. Retrieved from https://aiatsis.gov.au/research/research-ethics/research-ethics-guidelines

Baháʼí International Community. (n.d.). *Interfaith Dialogue*. Retrieved from https://www.bahai.org/action/social-action/interfaith-dialogue.

Baháʼuʼlláh. (1993). *Tablets of Baháʼuʼlláh, Revealed after the Kitáb-i-Aqdas* (1st Pocket-Sized ed.). Wilmette, IL. Baháʼí Publishing.

Bakhtin, M. M., et al. (2011). *The Dialogic Imagination: Four Essays* (18th Paperback Printing). Austin. University of Texas Press.

Baran-Łucarz, M. (2014). The Link between Pronunciation Anxiety and Willingness to Communicate in the Foreign-Language Classroom: The Polish EFL Context. *The Canadian Modern Language Review*, 70(4), 445–73. DOI.org (Crossref), https://doi.org/10.3138/cmlr.2666.

Barton, D., Burkhart, J., & Sever, C. (2010). *The Business English Teacher: Professional Principles and Practical Procedures*. Delta Publishing.

Bell English. (2021). Retrieved from https://www.bellenglish.com/about-bell/ (accessed 16 July 2021).

Berger, A. (1996). Jewish debating traditions. In D. Frank & O. Leaman (Eds.), *The Cambridge Companion to Medieval Jewish Philosophy* (pp. 17–33). Cambridge. Cambridge University Press.

Bradberry, T., & Greaves, J. (2009). *Emotional Intelligence 2.0.* Talent Smart.

Branden, K. V. D. (Ed.). (2006). *Task-Based Language Education: From Theory to Practice.* Cambridge. Cambridge University Press.

Brink, A. (2014). Aboriginal oral traditions and storytelling. In A. F. Blackstock (Ed.), *Colonial Contexts and Postcolonial Theologies: Story Weaving in the Asia-Pacific* (pp. 201–14). London. Palgrave Macmillan.

British Educational Research Association. (2018). *Ethical Guidelines for Educational Research.* BERA. https://www.bera.ac.uk/publication/ethical-guidelines-for-educational-research-2018

Brown, H. D. (1999). A map of the terrain. In J. Arnold (Ed.), *Affect in Language Learning* (pp. 1–24). Cambridge. Cambridge University Press.

Brunskill, J. (2018). *Why Social and Emotional Learning Skills Are as Important as Knowledge. Times Educational Supplement.* Retrieved from https://www.tes.com/news/why-social-and-emotional-learning-skills-are-important-knowledge-sponsored-article.

Buriro, G. A. B., & Siddiqui, J. A. (2015). Investigating Learner Beliefs as EFL Speaking Anxiety Factor at Public Sector Universities in Sindh. *International Journal of Arts and Humanities*, 43(43), 67–84.

Burns, A. (2010). *Doing Action Research in English Language Teaching: A Guide for Practitioners.* London. Routledge.

Busygina, N. P., & Yaroshevskaya, S. V. (2020). Cultural-Historical Psychology as a Theory of Subjectivity in the Works of F. González Rey. *Cultural-Historical Psychology*, 16(1), 68–77. DOI.org (Crossref), https://doi.org/10.17759/chp.2020160107.

Buswell Jr., R. E. (2004). Encyclopedia of Buddhism, p. 161. New York. Macmillan Reference USA. ISBN 978-0-02-865910-7.

Cambridge English. (2021). *Syllabus and Assessment Guidelines.* Retrieved from https://www.cambridgeenglish.org/Images/21816-celta-syllabus.pdf (accessed 9 August 2021).

Cambridge University Press. (2021). *Cambridge Online Dictionary.* Retrieved from https://dictionary.cambridge.org/dictionary/english/english-as-a-foreign-language (accessed 14 July 2021).

Campos-Lima, E. (22 November 2021). To Understand Our Battles over Critical Race Theory and Liberation Theology, Look to Brazil's Fight over Paulo Freire's Legacy. *America: The Jesuit Review.* Retrieved from https://www.americamagazine.org/politics-society/2021/11/22/paulo-freire-brazil-pedagogy-oppressed-241593.

Celce-Murcia, M., & Brinton, D. M. (2014). *Teaching English as a Second or Foreign Language* (4th ed.). Boston. National Geographic Learning: Heinle Cengage Learning.

Chomsky, N. (1988). *Language and Problems of Knowledge: The Managua Lectures.* Cambridge, MA. MIT Press.

Chomsky, N. (2002). *Democracy & Education.* London. Routledge.

Chomsky, N., & Halle, M. (1965). Some Controversial Questions in Phonological Theory. *Journal of Linguistics*, 1(2), 97–138. DOI.org (Crossref), https://doi.org/10.1017/S0022226700001134.

Chomsky, N., & Skinner, B. F. (1959). Verbal Behavior. *Language*, 35(1), 26. DOI.org (Crossref), https://doi.org/10.2307/411334.

Cinganotto, L. (2019). Debate as a Teaching Strategy for Language Learning. *Lingue e Linguaggi*, 107–25. Retrieved from https://www.researchgate.net/publication/336836038_DEBATE_AS_A_TEACHING_STRATEGY_FOR_LANGUAGE_LEARNING_Lingue_e_Linguaggi.

Coffin, C., et al. (2009). *Exploring English Grammar: From Formal to Functional.* London. Routledge.

Cohen, A. (1995). *Everyman's Talmud: The Major Teachings of the Rabbinic Sages.* Bn Publishing. New York. Schocken.

Cohen, L., et al. (2007). *Research Methods in Education* (6th ed.). London. Routledge.

Colbert, K. (1995). Enhancing Critical Thinking Ability through Debate. *Contemporary Argumentation and Debate*, 16, 52–72.

Council of Europe. (2021). *Common European Framework of Reference for Languages.* Retrieved from https://www.coe.int/en/web/common-european-framework-reference-languages (accessed 6 August 2020).

Council of Europe. (2021). *Foreign Language Learning.* Retrieved from https://ec.europa.eu/eurostat/statistics-explained/index.php?title=Foreign_language_learning_statistics.

Curran, C. A. (1969). *Religious Values in Counselling & Psychotherapy.* New York. Sheen & Ward.

Curran, C. A. (1972). *Counseling-Learning: A Whole-Person Model for Education.* New York. Grune & Stratton.

Curran, C. A. (1976). *Counseling-Learning in Second Languages.* New York. Apple River Press.

Curran, C. A. (1978). *Understanding: A Necessary Ingredient in Human Belonging.* New York. Apple River Press.

Dewaele, J. M., et al. (2019). The Flowering of Positive Psychology in Foreign Language Teaching and Acquisition Research. *Frontiers in Psychology*, 10, 2128. DOI.org (Crossref), https://doi.org/10.3389/fpsyg.2019.02128.

Dewey, J. (1938). *Experience and Education.* New York. Free Press.

Diggs, J. (2008). Activity theory of aging. In S. J. Loue & M. Sajatovic (Eds.), *Encyclopedia of Aging and Public Health.* Springer. DOI.org (Crossref), https://doi.org/10.1007/978-0-387-33754-8_9.

Dörnyei, Z. (2018). *Safe Speaking Environments.* Retrieved from https://www.youtube.com/watch?v=-wDmI-DUt-c.

Dörnyei, Z., & Ryan, S. (2015). *The Psychology of the Language Learner Revisited.* London. Routledge, Taylor & Francis Group.

Dornyei, Z., & Ushioda, E. (2021). *Teaching and Researching Motivation.* London. Routledge.

Dufva, H. (2013). Language learning as dialogue and participation in problem-based learning for the 21st century, new practices and learning environments. In E. Christiansen, L. Kuure, A. Mørch, & B. Lindström (Eds.), *Problem-Based Learning for the 21st Century* (pp. 51–67). Aalborg. Aalborg Universitetsforlag.

Durlak, J. A. (Ed.). (2015). *Handbook of Social and Emotional Learning: Research and Practice*. New York. The Guilford Press.

Edelstein, E. (2020). *English Syntax: A Minimalist Account of Structure and Variation*. Edinburgh. Edinburgh University Press.

Effiong, O. (2015). Getting Them Speaking: Classroom Social Factors and Foreign Language Anxiety. *TESOL Journal*, 7(1), 132–61. DOI.org (Crossref), https://doi.org/10.1002/tesj.194.

Eknath, E. (2019). *The Bhagavad Gita*. Tomales, CA. Nilgiri Press.

Elhassan, I., & Adam, M. (2017). The Impact of Dialogic Teaching on English Language Learners' Speaking and Thinking Skills. *Arab World English Journal*, 8(4), 49–67. DOI.org (Crossref), https://doi.org/10.24093/awej/vol8no4.4.

Elkhafaifi, H. (2005). Listening Comprehension and Anxiety in the Arabic Language Classroom. *The Modern Language Journal*, 89(2), 206–20. DOI.org (Crossref), https://doi.org/10.1111/j.1540-4781.2005.00275.x.

Ellis, R. (2003). *Task-Based Learning*. Oxford. Oxford University Press.

Ellis, R. (2013). *Second Language Acquisition*. Oxford. Oxford University Press.

El Sakka, S. M. F. (2019). Explicit Affective Strategy Instruction to Develop Speaking Performance of Egyptian EFL University Students. *English Language Teaching*, 12(4), 85. DOI.org (Crossref), https://doi.org/10.5539/elt.v12n4p85.

Esslemont, J. E. (2006). *Bahá'u'lláh and the New Era* (4th rev. ed.). Wilmette, IL. Bahá'í Publishing.

Evans, R., & Jones, D. (2007). Perspectives on Oracy – towards a Theory of Practice. *Early Child Development and Care*, 177(6–7), 557–67. DOI.org (Crossref), https://doi.org/10.1080/03004430701424938.

Fakhry, M. (1983). *A History of Islamic Philosophy*. New York. Columbia University Press.

Farid-Arbab, S. (2016). *Moral Empowerment: In Quest of a Pedagogy*. Wilmette, IL. Bahá'í Publishing.

Ferster, C. B., & Skinner, B. F. (1957). *Schedules of Reinforcement*. Appleton-Century-Crofts.

Feser, E. (2009). *Aquinas*. New York. Simon and Schuster.

Forsyth, D. R. (2006). *Group Dynamics*. Belmont, CA. Thomson/Wadsworth.

Fowler, J. (2012). *Hinduism: Beliefs and Practices*. Portland, OR. Sussex Academic Press.

Fox, M. V. (2008). *The Cambridge Companion to Jewish Studies*. Cambridge. Cambridge University Press.

Freeley, A. J., & Steinberg, D. L. (2014). *Argumentation and Debate: Critical Thinking for Reasoned Decision Making*. Belmont, CA. Wadsworth.

Freire, P. (1972). *Pedagogy of the Oppressed*. London. Continuum.

Freire, P. (1974). *Education for Critical Consciousness*. New York. Sheed & Ward.

Gánem-Gutiérrez, G. A., & Nogués Meléndez, C. (2013). Mediating the Development of L2 Oral Performance through Dynamic Assessment: Focusing on the Metalinguistic Dimension. In K. Roehr & G. A. Gánem-Gutiérrez (Eds.), *The Metalinguistic Dimension in Instructed Second Language Learning*. Advances in Instructed Second Language Acquisition Research (pp. 195–219). London. Bloomsbury. ISBN 9781441160898.

Gattegno, C. (2010). *Teaching Foreign Languages in Schools: The Silent Way*. Repr. New York. New York Educational Solutions Worlwide.

Gaunt, A., & Stott, A. (2019). *Transform Teaching and Learning through Talk: The Oracy Imperative*. Lanham, MD. Rowman & Littlefield.

Gethin, R. (1998). *Foundations of Buddhism*. Oxford. Oxford University Press.

Glassman, W. E., & Hadad, M. (2013). *Approaches to Psychology* (6th ed.). London. Mcgraw-Hill Higher Education.

Goldberg, A. E. (1995). *Constructions: A Construction Grammar Approach to Argument Structure*. Chicago, IL. University of Chicago Press.

Golden, J. L. (2003). *The Rhetoric of Western Thought: From the Mediterranean World to the Global Setting*. Dubuque, IA. Kendall/Hunt.

González-Lloret, M., et al. (2021). Role of Technology in Language Teaching and Learning amid the Crisis Generated by the COVID-19 Pandemic. *Íkala*, 26(3), 477–82. DOI.org (Crossref), https://doi.org/10.17533/udea.ikala.v26n3a01.

González Rey, F. L. (2019). Subjectivity and Discourse: Complementary Topics for a Critical Psychology. *Culture & Psychology*, 25(2), 178–94. DOI.org (Crossref), https://doi.org/10.1177/1354067X18754338.

Guthrie, W. K. C. (1978). *An Introduction to Greek Philosophy: Socrates, Plato, and Aristotle* (Vol. 1). Cambridge. Cambridge University Press.

Habermas, J. (1972). *Knowledge and Human Interests* (trans. J. Shapiro). London. Heinemann.

Habermas, J. (1974). *Theory and Practice* (trans. J. Viertel). London. Heinemann.

Halliday, M. A. K. (1976). *Explorations in the Functions of Language*. London. Edward Arnold.

Halliday, M. A. K., & Matthiessen, C. M. I. M. (2006). *Construing Experience through Meaning: A Language-Based Approach to Cognition*. London. Continuum.

Han, T., Tanriöver, A. S., & Şahan, Ö. (2016). EFL Students' and Teachers' Attitudes toward Foreign Language Speaking Anxiety: A Look at NESTs and Non-NESTs. *International Education Studies*, 9(3), 1–11.

Harmer, J. (2013). *The Practice of English Language Teaching: With DVD* (4th ed., 8th impression). London. Pearson Education.

Harris, R. A. (2021). *The Linguistics Wars*. Oxford. Oxford University Press.

Hawkins, R. (2001). *Second Language Syntax: A Generative Introduction*. London. Blackwell Publishers.

Hayes, M. A., & Gearon, L. (Eds.). (2002). *Contemporary Catholic Education*. Gracewing.

Holmes, A. G. D. (2020). Researcher Positionality – A Consideration of Its Influence and Place in Qualitative Research – A New Researcher Guide. *Shanlax International Journal of Education*, 8(4), 1–10. DOI.org (Crossref), https://doi.org/10.34293/education.v8i4.3232.

Horkheimer, M. (1972). *Critical Theory; Selected Essays*. New York. Herder and Herder.

Howatt, A. P. R., & Smith, R. (2014). The History of Teaching English as a Foreign Language, from a British and European Perspective. *Language & History*, 57(1), 75–95. DOI.org (Crossref), https://doi.org/10.1179/1759753614Z.00000000028.

Hudson, R. A. (2010). *An Introduction to Word Grammar.* Cambridge. Cambridge University Press.

Hughes, R. (2002). *Teaching & Researching Speaking.* London. Routledge.

Hughes, R., & Szczepek-Reed, B. (2017). *Teaching & Researching Speaking* (3rd ed.). London. Routledge.

Hunter, J. (2012). 'Small Talk': Developing Fluency, Accuracy, and Complexity in Speaking. *ELT Journal*, 66(1), 30–41. DOI.org (Crossref), https://doi.org/10.1093/elt/ccq093.

Iman, J. N. (2017). Debate Instruction in EFL Classroom: Impacts on the Critical Thinking and Speaking Skill. *International Journal of Instruction*, 10(4), 87–108. DOI.org (Crossref), https://doi.org/10.12973/iji.2017.1046a.

Inlingua. (2021). Retrieved from https://www.inlingua.com/ (accessed 16 July 2021).

Inoue, N., & Nakano, M. (2004). *The benefits and costs of participating in competitive debate activities: Differences between Japanese and American college students.* Paper presented at Wake Forest University/International Society for the Study of Argumentation 'Venice Argumentation Conference', Venice, Italy.

International House. (2021). Retrieved from https://ihworld.com/ (accessed 16 July 2021).

Jackendoff, R. (2002). *Foundations of Language: Brain, Meaning, Grammar, Evolution.* Oxford. Oxford University Press.

Jindal, K. (2017). *Hinduism and Interfaith Dialogue: Perspectives from Environmental Ethics.* London. Palgrave Macmillan.

Jones, S. M., & Bouffard, S. M. (2012). Social and Emotional Learning in Schools: From Programs to Strategies and Commentaries. *Social Policy Report*, 26(4), 1–33. DOI.org (Crossref), https://doi.org/10.1002/j.2379-3988.2012.tb00073.x.

Jordan, D., & Streets, D. (1973). Guiding the Process of Becoming: The ANISA Theories of Curriculum and Teaching. *World Order*, 7(4), 29–40. Retrieved from http://www.edpsycinteractive.org/anisa/curriculum/streets_jordan_becoming.pdf.

Katz, S. T. (2006). The Disputations of Barcelona and Tortosa Reconsidered. *The Jewish Quarterly Review*, 96(4), 615–46.

Kennedy, Ruth R. (November 2009). The Power of In-Class Debates. *Active Learning in Higher Education*, 10(3), 225–36. DOI.org (Crossref), https://doi.org/10.1177/1469787409343186.

Kern, R. (2010). *Literacy and Language Teaching.* Oxford. Oxford University Press.

Kerr, F. (2002). *After Aquinas: Versions of Thomism.* London. Blackwell Publishers.

Kessler, G. (March 2018). Technology and the Future of Language Teaching. *Foreign Language Annals*, 51(1), 205–18. DOI.org (Crossref), https://doi.org/10.1111/flan.12318.

Khan, I., et al. (October 2020). A Critical Appraisal of Interreligious Dialogue in Islam. *SAGE Open*, 10(4), p. 215824402097056. DOI.org (Crossref), https://doi.org/10.1177/2158244020970560.

Khan, Z. A. (May 2010). The Effects of Anxiety on Cognitive Processing in English Language Learning. *English Language Teaching*, 3(2), 199. DOI.org (Crossref), https://doi.org/10.5539/elt.v3n2p199.

Klostermaier, K. (2007). *A Survey of Hinduism*. Albany. SUNY Press.

Kolstoe. (1985). *Consultation: A Light of Guidance*. Oxford. George Ronald.

Krashen, S. D. (1985). *The Input Hypothesis: Issues and Implications*. London. Longman.

Krashen, S. D., & Terrell, Tracy D. (2000). *The Natural Approach: Language Acquisition in the Classroom* (1st ed.). New York. Phoenix Press.

Kubanyiova, M. (2018). *Creating a Safe Speaking Environment. Cambridge Papers in ELT Series*. Cambridge. Cambridge University Press.

Küçük, H. (2016). Islamic Debates on Democracy and Human Rights. *The Review of Faith & International Affairs*, 14(3), 1–9. DOI.org (Crossref), 10.1080/15570274.2016.1208354.

Kumaravadivelu, B. (1994). The Postmethod Condition: (E)Merging Strategies for Second/Foreign Language Teaching. *TESOL Quarterly*, 28(1), 27. DOI.org (Crossref), https://doi.org/10.2307/3587197.

Kumaravadivelu, B. (2003). *Beyond Methods: Macrostrategies for Language Teaching*. London. Yale University Press.

Lai, H.-Y.T. (2013). The Motivation of Learners of English as a Foreign Language Revisited. *International Education Studies*, 6(10), 90–101. DOI.org (Crossref), https://doi.org/10.5539/ies.v6n10p90.

Lantolf, J. P., & Thorne, S. L. (2006). *Sociocultural Theory and the Genesis of Second Language Development*. Oxford. Oxford University Press.

Larsen-Freeman, D., & Anderson, M. (2011). *Techniques and Principles in Language Teaching* (3rd ed.). Oxford. Oxford University Press.

Leaman, O. (2013). *An Introduction to Medieval Islamic Philosophy*. Cambridge. Cambridge University Press.

Levin, R. A., & Hines, L. M. (2003). Educational Television, Fred Rogers, and the History of Education. *History of Education Quarterly*, 43(2), 262–75. DOI.org (Crossref), https://doi.org/10.1111/j.1748-5959.2003.tb00123.x.

Lewis, M. (1993). *The Lexical Approach: The State of ELT and a Way Forward*. Hove. Language Teaching Publications.

Li, X., Liu, Q., & Cai, H. (2021). The Impact of COVID-19 on Online Education: A Comparative Study. *Journal of Educational Technology Development and Exchange*, 14(1), 1–14.

Liu, D. (2018). The Benefits of One-to-One Online English Language Learning: Perceptions of Chinese Learners. *Journal of Educational Technology Development and Exchange*, 11(1), 1–14.

Liu, M., & Jackson, J. (2011). Reticence and anxiety in oral English lessons: A case study in China. In D. Nunan (Ed.), *Learning to Teach English in the Secondary School: A Companion to School Experience* (pp. 76–89). London. Palgrave Macmillan. DOI.org (Crossref), 10.1057/9780230299481_6.

Liu, M., & Li, X. (2019). Changes in and Effects of Anxiety on English Test Performance in Chinese Postgraduate EFL Classrooms. *Education Research International* (1):1–11. DOI.org (Crossref), https://doi.org/10.1155/2019/7213925.

Lozanov, G. (1978). *Suggestology and Outlines of Suggestopedy*. Gordon and Breach.

Luria, A. R. (1994). *Cognitive Development: Its Cultural and Social Foundations* (M. Cole, Ed.). Harvard. Harvard University Press.

Maslow, A. H. (1999). *Toward a Psychology of Being* (3rd ed.). London. J. Wiley & Sons.

Matusov, E. (2023). The Educational Regime of the Bakhtinian Dialogue. *Dialogic Pedagogy: An International Online Journal*, 11(1), E1–15. DOI.org (Crossref), https://doi.org/10.5195/dpj.2023.561.

McAdams, D. P. (June 2001). The Psychology of Life Stories. *Review of General Psychology*, 5(2), 100–22. DOI.org (Crossref), https://doi.org/10.1037/1089-2680.5.2.100.

McAdams, D. P., & Adler, J. (2006). How does personality develop? In D. K. Mroczek & T. Little (Eds.), *Handbook of Personality Development* (pp. 469–92). Erlbaum.

McBrien, R. P. (2013). *Catholicism* (Completely Rev. and Updated ed.). London. Harper Collins.

McCormick, M. P., et al. (2015). Social-Emotional Learning and Academic Achievement: Using Causal Methods to Explore Classroom-Level Mechanisms. *AERA Open*, 1(3), 233285841560395. DOI.org (Crossref), https://doi.org/10.1177/2332858415603959.

Meaningful and Distinctive Conversations | *Baha'i Blog*. (2013). Retrieved from https://www.bahaiblog.net/articles/bahai-life/meaningful-and-distinctive-conversations/ (accessed 13 October 2023).

Meddings, L., & Thornbury, S. (2010). *Teaching Unplugged: Dogme in English Language Teaching*. Delta Publishing.

Meigouni, E., & Shirkhani, S. (2020). Oral Communication Strategies Used by Iranian EFL Learners and Their Relationship with the Learners' Self-efficacy Beliefs and Anxiety Level. *Research in English Language Pedagogy*, 8(1): 1–20. Retrieved from http://relp.khuisf.ac.ir/article_669075_bd2632c5afceaab56220cbc01b9375e9.pdf.

Mercer, S. (2018). Psychology for Language Learning: Spare a Thought for the Teacher. *Language Teaching*, 51(4), 504–25. DOI.org (Crossref), https://doi.org/10.1017/S0261444817000258.

Meshcheryakova, R. (2016). Perezhivanie: From the Dictionary of Psychology. *Mind, Culture, and Activity*, 23(4), 272–3. DOI.org (Crossref), https://doi.org/10.1080/10749039.2016.1225310.

Momen, M. (1999). *The Phenomenon of Religion: A Thematic Approach*. London. Oneworld.

Moskowitz, G. (1978). *Caring and Sharing in the Foreign Language Class: A Sourcebook on Humanistic Techniques* (1st ed.). Heinle and Heinle Publishers.

Nastional Scientific Council on the Developing Child. (2005/2014). *Excessive Stress Disrupts the Architecture of the Developing Brain: Working Paper No. 3*. Retrieved from www.developingchild.harvard.edu.

Nguyen, N. Q., & Bui Phu, H. (2020). The Dogme Approach: A Radical Perspective in Second Language Teaching in the Post-Methods Era. *Journal of Language and Education*, 6(3), 173–84. DOI.org (Crossref), https://doi.org/10.17323/jle.2020.10563.

Noll, M. A., & Nystrom, C. C. (2016). *Thinking like a Christian: Understanding and Living a Biblical Worldview*. Brentwood, TN. B&H Publishing Group.

Norton, B. (2013). *Identity and Language Learning: Extending the Conversation* (2nd ed.). Bristol. Multilingual Matters.

Nunan, D. (2004). *Task-Based Learning*. Cambridge. Cambridge University Press.

Oaklander, N. L. (2014). *Debates in the Metaphysics of Time*. London. Bloomsbury.

Olson, R. E. (2011). *The Story of Christian Theology: Twenty Centuries of Tradition & Reform*. Downers Grove, IL. InterVarsity Press.

Open University. (2003). *Research Methods in Education*. Milton Keynes. Open University Press.

O'Reilly, K. (2009). *Key Concepts in Ethnography*. London. SAGE.

Organisation for Economic Co-operation and Development (OECD). (2013). *Inchiesta sugli competenze sulle adulti primi risultati* (Research into Adult Skills: First Results): *Nota Paese: Italia* (Country Notes: Italy). Retrieved from https://www.oecd.org/skills/piaac/Country%20note%20-%20Italy%20(ITA).pdf (accessed 11 August 2021).

Organization for Economic Co-operation and Development (OECD). (2015). *Skills for Social Progress: The Power of Social and Emotional Skills*. Retrieved from https://www.oecd.org/education/school/UPDATED%20Social%20and%20Emotional%20Skills%20-%20Well-being,%20connectedness%20and%20success.pdf%20(website).pdf.

Organization for Economic Co-operation and Development (OECD). (2019). *Skills Matter: Additional Results from the Survey of Adult Skills*. DOI.org (Crossref), https://doi.org/10.1787/1f029d8f-en.

Organization for Economic Co-operation and Development (OECD). (2021). *Social-Emotional Skills Study*. Retrieved from https://www.oecd.org/education/ceri/social-emotional-skills-study/.

Our English Learning Method – Wall Street English. (n.d.). Retrieved from https://www.wallstreetenglish.com/blog/english-learning-method (accessed 13 October 2023).

Perdue, D. (1992). *Debate in Tibetan Buddhism*. Boston. Snow Lion Publications.

Perdue, D. (2014). *The Course in Buddhist Reasoning and Debate: An Asian Approach to Analytical Thinking Drawn from Indian and Tibetan Sources*. Snow Lion Publications.

Pienemann, M., & Kessler, Jörg-U. (Ed.). (2011). *Studying Processability Theory: An Introductory Textbook*. Amsterdam. John Benjamins Publishing Company.

Pishghadam, R. (May 2016). *Emotioncy, extraversion, and anxiety in willingness to communicate in English*. In Proceedings of the 5th International Conference on Language, Education, and Innovation (pp. 1–5). The Interdisciplinary Circle of Science, Arts, and Innovation. Retrieved from https://icsai.org/procarch/5iclei/5iclei-4.html.

Plato, & Tarrant, H. (1954). *The Last Days of Socrates: Euthyphro, the Apology, Crito, Phaedo*. London. Penguin Books.

Plato, & Waterfield, R. (2008). *Republic*. Oxford. Oxford University Press.

Pondiscio, R. (2021). *The Unexamined Rise of Therapeutic Education: How Social Emotional Learning Extends K-12 Education's Reach into Students' Lives and Expands Teachers' Roles*. Conservative Education Reform Network.

Prabhavathy, P. (2012). ELT with Specific Regard to Humanistic Approach. *IOSR Journal of Humanities and Social Science*, 1(1), 38–9. DOI.org (Crossref), https://doi.org/10.9790/0837-0113839.

Ram-Prasad, C. (Ed.). (2007). *Encountering Religions: Hinduism*. London. Equinox Publishing.

Ray, R. (2018). The history and practice of Buddhist debating in Tibet. In R. Ray (Ed.), *Buddhist Debates in Contemporary Tibet* (pp. 1–17). London. Routledge.

Richards, J. C. (2010). *Communicative Language Teaching*. Cambridge. Cambridge University Press. DOI.org (Crossref), https://doi.org/10.1017/CBO9780511667305.018.

Richards, J. C., & Rodgers, T. S. (2014). *Approaches and Methods in Language Teaching* (3rd ed.). Cambridge. Cambridge University Press.

Rizvi, S. (2007). Reason and Inspiration in Islam: Theology, Philosophy and Mysticism in Islamic Thought. *Journal of Islamic Studies*, 18(3), 411–13. DOI.org (Crossref), https://doi.org/10.1093/jis/etm034.

Roehr, K., & Ganem-Gutierrez, G. A. (2013). *The Metalinguistic Dimension in Instructed Second Language Learning*. London. Bloomsbury Academic.

Rose, D., & Martin, J. R. (2012). *Learning to Write, Reading to Learn: Genre, Knowledge and Pedagogy in the Sydney School*. London. Equinox Publishing.

Rubio, F. (Ed.). (2007). *Self-Esteem and Foreign Language Learning*. Cambridge. Cambridge Scholars Publishing.

Rybold, G., & Harvey-Smith, N. (2013). *Speaking, Listening and Understanding. English Language Debate for Non-native Speakers*. London. International Debate Education Association.

Sajjad R. (2007). Reason and Inspiration in Islam: Theology, Philosophy and Mysticism in Islamic Thought: Essays in Honour of Hermann Landolt. *Journal of Islamic Studies*, 18(3), 411–13.

Saslow, L. R., et al. (2014). Speaking under Pressure: Low Linguistic Complexity Is Linked to High Physiological and Emotional Stress Reactivity. *Psychophysiology*, 51(3), 257–66. DOI.org (Crossref), https://doi.org/10.1111/psyp.12171.

Schechter, S. (2018). Jewish Dialogue and Debate: The Tradition of Dispute in Judaism. *The Jewish Quarterly Review*, 108(3), 403–22. DOI.org (Crossref), 10.1353/jqr.2018.0020.

Scrivener, J. (2005). *Learning Teaching: A Guidebook for English Language Teachers* (2nd ed.). London. Macmillan.

Setiawan, H. (2018). The Use of Group Investigation Technique in Improving Students' Speaking Skill at Tridinanti University of Palembang. *Edukasi Lingua Sastra*, 16(1), May 2018, 91–99. DOI.org (Crossref), https://doi.org/10.47637/elsa.v16i1.88.

Setiyadi, A. B., Mahpul, M., & Wicaksono, A. (2019). Exploring Motivational Orientations of English as Foreign Language (EFL) Learners: A Case Study in Indonesia. *South African Journal of Education*, 39(1), 1–12. DOI.org (Crossref), https://doi.org/10.15700/saje.v39n1a1500.

Sharma, C. (2014). *A Critical Survey of Indian Philosophy*. Delhi. Motilal Banarsidass Publishers.

Skinner. (1957). *Verbal Behaviour*. La Jolla, CA. Copley Press.

Snider, A., & Schnurer, M. (2002). *Many Sides: Debate across the Curriculum*. New York. International Debate Education Association.

Spaces of Consultation. (n.d.). Retrieved from https://www.bahai.org/action/institutional-capacity/spaces-consultation (accessed 13 October 2023).

Stanford Encyclopedia of Philosophy. (n.d.). *Ancient Greek Philosophy*. Retrieved from https://plato.stanford.edu/entries/ancient-greek-philosophy/

Stevick, E. W. (1980). *Teaching Languages: A Way and Ways*. Rowley, MA. Newbury House Publishers.

Stevick, E. W. (1990). *Humanism in Language Teaching: A Critical Perspective*. Oxford. Oxford University Press.

Swain, M. (2005). The output hypothesis: Theory and research. In E. Hinkel (Ed.), *Handbook of Research in Second Language Teaching and Learning* (pp. 471–84). London. Routledge.

Swain, M., & Lapkin, S. (1995). Problems in Output and the Cognitive Processes They Generate: A Step towards Second Language Learning. *Applied Linguistics*, 16(3), 371–91. DOI.org (Crossref), https://doi.org/10.1093/applin/16.3.371.

Swan, M. (2012). *Thinking about Language Teaching: Selected Articles 1982–2011*. Oxford. Oxford University Press.

Tawalbeh, T. I., & Al-Asmari, A. A. (2015). Instructors' Perceptions and Barriers of Learner-Centered Instruction in English at the University Level. *Higher Education Studies*, 5(2), 38–51. DOI.org (Crossref), https://doi.org/10.5539/hes.v5n2p38.

Teesside University. (2020). *Policy, Procedures and Guidelines for Research Ethics*. Retrieved from https://extra.tees.ac.uk/sites/publicdocuments/Legal%20and%20Governance%20Services/Policy,%20Procedures%20and%20Guidelines%20for%20Research%20Ethics.pdf.

Thiriau, C. (2017). Global Teaching Speaking Survey: The Results. *World of Better Learning*. Retrieved from https://www.cambridge.org/elt/blog/2017/11/06/teaching-speaking-survey-results/.

Tomasello, M. (2003). *Constructing a Language: A Usage-Based Theory of Language Acquisition*. Harvard. Harvard University Press.

Toubot, A. M., Hock Seng, G., & Binti Atan Abdullah, A. (2018). Examining Levels and Factors of Speaking Anxiety among EFL Libyan English Undergraduate Students. *International Journal of Applied Linguistics and English Literature*, 7(5), 47. DOI.org (Crossref), https://doi.org/10.7575/aiac.ijalel.v.7n.5p.47.

Tsai, C.-C. (2013). The Impact of Foreign Language Anxiety, Tests Anxiety, and Self-Efficacy among Senior High School Students in Taiwan. *International Journal of English Language and Linguistics Research*, 1(2), 31–47.

Tsai, C.-C. (2018). The Effects of Communication Strategy Training on EFL Speaking Anxiety and Speaking Strategy among the Community College Adult Learners in Taiwan. *International Forum of Teaching and Studies*, 14(2). Retrieved from http://americanscholarspress.us/journals/IFST/pdf/IFOTS-2-2018/IFOTS-v14n2art1.pdf.

Underhill, A. (1989). Process in Humanistic Education. *ELT Journal*, 43(4), 250–60. DOI.org (Crossref), https://doi.org/10.1093/elt/43.4.250.

Vygotsky, L. (1978). *Mind in Society: The Development of Higher Psychological Processes*. Harvard. Harvard University Press.

Wall Street English. Our English Learning Method – Wall Street English. (n.d.). Retrieved from https://www.wallstreetenglish.com/blog/english-learning-method (accessed 13 October 2023).

Warren, P. (2013). *Introducing Psycholinguistics*. Cambridge. Cambridge University Press.

WEF. (2021). *Why You Need Emotional Intelligence*. Retrieved from https://www.weforum.org/agenda/2017/02/why-you-need-emotional-intelligence.

White, L. (2013). *Second Language Acquisition and Universal Grammar*. Cambridge. Cambridge University Press.

Whong, M. (2011). *Language Teaching: Linguistic Theory in Practice*. Edinburgh. Edinburgh University Press.

Wilkins, D. A. (1976). *Notional Syllabuses*. Oxford. Oxford University Press.

Williams, M. (1994). Motivation in foreign and second language learning: An interactive perspective. *Educational Psychology*, 91, 76–97.

Willis, J., & Willis, D. (2007). *Doing Task-Based Teaching*. Oxford. Oxford University Press.

Wu, K. H. (2010). The Relationship between Language Learners' Anxiety and Learning Strategy in the CLT Classrooms. *International Education Studies*, 3(1), 174. DOI.org (Crossref), https://doi.org/10.5539/ies.v3n1p174.

Yan, J. X., & Horwitz, E. K. (2008). Learners' Perceptions of How Anxiety Interacts with Personal and Instructional Factors to Influence Their Achievement in English: A Qualitative Analysis of EFL Learners in China. *Language Learning*, 58(1), 151–83. DOI.org (Crossref), https://doi.org/10.1111/j.1467-9922.2007.00437.x.

Zayed, J., & Al-Ghamdi, H. (2019). The Relationships among Affective Factors in Learning EFL: A Study of the Saudi Setting. *English Language Teaching*, 12(9), 105. DOI.org (Crossref), https://doi.org/10.5539/elt.v12n9p105.

Index

ability
    to communicate 100
    to construct knowledge 38
    critical thinking 12, 26, 30, 49, 52, 104
    to employ strategies & approaches 55
    to express 99
    insecurity 74
    language 94, 98, 123
    to learn a second language 52
    speaking 44, 47, 100, 103
accuracy (*see* speaking)
adult Education 56, 120, 151
affect
    affective strategy 46
    benefits 49–50
    and cognition 82, 91
    of dialogic speaking 9, 35, 64
    and hierarchy of needs 147
    history of affect in Psychology and language teaching 50–54
    humanism 51–54
    management of discourse 97
    negative 10, 57, 58, 62, 64, 69, 73, 74, 75, 81, 83, 96, 97, 99, 100, 109, 113, 114, 120, 139
    positive 2, 3, 10, 17, 18, 45, 53, 58, 59, 64, 70, 74, 75, 76, 79, 84, 85, 89, 90, 91, 94, 95, 99, 102, 106, 107, 109, 113, 114, 118, 121, 122, 125, 145
    scale of positive and negative 84
    and self-actualization 89, 149
    social 47
affective filter hypothesis 17
agreeing 73
anxiety
    acquisition 60, 61
    cause of anxiety 59, 115
    increasing 62
    and learner attitude 62, 63, 115
    overcoming 62, 98
    preventing 57
    reducing 61, 113
    research into anxiety 60–61
    and self-confidence 62
    speaking 60, 61
    teacher as source 61
approaches to SLA 36, 37
Aristotle 7, 8, 11, 12, 26, 27, 30, 91

Baha'i faith 25, 29
Behaviourism 10, 57

Cambridge English 41
Catholicism 7, 29
CELTA 41, 47, 55, 118, 119, 125, 126
Chomsky 16, 22, 51
Christianity 28
classroom dynamics 7
classroom talk 102, 129
cognition
    and affect 88
    and communication 91
    and emotion 105
    and experience of 112, 117
    metacognition 82, 112, 117
collaboration 13, 33, 103, 129
Common European framework for languages 152
communicative dynamics 71, 72, 76, 121
community
    being in true community 116
    a community of interest 122, 148
    community language learning 18, 45
    and genuine communication 95
    as a living task-orientated experience 123
    mutual engagement and belonging 116
    partaking in a community 74
    role in a community of learners 5
    and the role of the teacher 96
competition 92, 98
comprehension
    and cognition 80, 81, 82
    difficulty in 83

Index

and engagement 91
and expression 75
improvement of 107
listening 38, 138
confidence
    and anxiety 62
    and fluency 31
    increased 12, 31, 32, 44, 50, 59, 62, 84
    influence of 62
    lack of self-confidence 46
    and low self-confidence 46
content
    course content 146
    curriculum content 46
    learner as source 59, 106
    and learning 30, 32
    relevance of content 30, 45, 49
convalidation 107
correction 44, 97, 107, 110, 112
counselling-learning approaches 18, 51, 53, 59, 93, 101, 115, 125
counsellor
    learner as 98, 99, 107, 108
    Teacher as 59, 98, 99, 125
cultural consciousness 45
cultural historical psychology 36
cultural historical theory 36, 37
cultural sensitivity 106
current affairs 68, 103
curriculum
    curriculum planning 51, 53, 54, 64, 67, 101, 121, 126, 146
    as elaborate itinerary 103

debating
    debating not as competitive 80, 92
    debating societies 26
    history of 23
    personal challenge of debating 89
declarative knowledge 19, 43
democratic 7, 9, 12, 13, 29, 32, 92
Dewey 37
dialectic 27, 29, 30, 33, 91, 126
dialogic speech 8, 12, 25, 28, 60
didactic 30, 91, 126
differentiation 23, 58, 96, 123, 153
disagreeing 73
discourse management 97

diversity
    and differentiation 58, 75, 97, 98
    teaching method as promoting diversity 54
dual practitioner 67, 128

educational Research 33, 151–52
emotional Intelligence 56
emotions 58, 62, 122
empathy 73, 94
errors 82, 97, 104, 110, 119
experiential 10, 11, 37, 61, 66, 69, 126, 127
expressing 27, 53, 71, 76, 82, 95, 112, 113, 134

face (loss of) 100, 104
feedback
    and I.R.F 44
    language feedback 44, 45, 87, 97, 102, 110, 138, 146
feelings
    expression of 10, 52
    learner's feelings 71, 72, 76
five stages of learning 94, 97, 108, 109, 114, 115, 126, 127
fluency
    improving 31, 44, 80, 110, 111
formal educational contexts 61

Greek 13, 26, 27, 28
Greek philosophy 27
group dynamics 1, 45, 92, 120, 124, 128, 137, 147

high school 63, 131, 133
higher education (universities) 15, 26, 31, 60, 62, 151
Hinduism 25, 26
holistic 3, 5, 10, 11, 20, 32, 33, 42, 43, 46, 50, 54, 56, 59, 60, 61, 63, 64, 65, 69, 70, 99, 101, 126, 127, 148, 151, 153

identity 58
Incarnate 93, 96, 97, 99, 100, 104, 114, 125
Incarnation 93, 97, 99, 103, 104
incidental learning 107
Independent stage of learning 99, 128
individual differences: individual differences in L2 acquisition 2, 76

input hypothesis 16, 39, 118
intellectual growth 73
interlanguage 2, 39, 44, 88
   and Curran's learning stages 109
   discourse aspects of interlanguage 8
   linguistic aspects of interlanguage 2, 8, 119
   social aspects of interlanguage 8
interpersonal 61
Islam 29

Judaism 26

L2 Self 60, 128
language Aptitude 63
language awareness 45, 117
language competence 41, 95, 110, 116
language schools 14, 42, 124, 152, 153
language systems 19, 23, 38, 117
learner
   learner attitudes 60, 63
   learner autonomy 17, 45, 80, 115
   learner needs 41, 104
   learner preferences 104
learning
   learning strategy 62
   peer 76, 78, 80, 87, 99, 101, 102, 105, 106, 108, 122, 129, 132, 148, 153
   self-directed 80
   stages of 109
linguistics 14, 15, 16, 17, 42, 43, 52, 55, 57
   applied linguistics 14, 57
   Chomsky 16, 51
   cognitive & functional 17
   formal 16, 42, 43
   sociolinguistics 42
   theoretical 43
listening
   non-judgmental 73

metacognition 82, 112, 117
metalinguistic 82, 83, 117, 118, 119, 148
methods
   the audiolingual method 15, 21, 42
   Berlitz method 14, 42
   the classical method 13
   direct method 14
   grammar-translation method 13, 14, 21, 43, 45, 62, 129
   the lexical approach 22, 131
   the multiple line of approach 15
   the natural method 14, 16
   the oral method 15
   the silent way 18, 52
   suggestapedia 18, 52
   Task based learning 21
   total physical response 52
Middle Ages 8, 26
middle school 131, 132, 133
mistakes 18, 46, 62, 104

Negotiated syllabus 148
noticing 47, 82, 117, 119

oracy 8, 21
output hypothesis 21, 118

patience 95, 129
pedagogy
   pedagogical shift 46, 61, 66, 68, 73, 74, 75, 92, 99, 102, 115
perezhivanie 37, 89, 128
personal growth 12, 60, 72, 87, 89, 99, 109, 114, 124, 126
   as 'I-myself engagement' 103
   I – myself – other 88
   as Incongruent 100
   as Redemption 99, 100, 114, 125, 127
Plato 7, 26, 27
positive psychology 2, 37, 55
post-methods era 20, 21, 56
Protestantism 28

respect 63, 72, 73, 94, 95, 100, 120, 127
Reversal stage 99
role of L1 16, 19, 20, 53

sacrifice 59, 99
safe-speaking spaces 129
scaffolding 22, 52, 99
scientism 11, 32, 43, 50
secondary schools 65
self-actualization 89, 95, 103, 108, 124, 149
self-esteem 32, 50, 57, 59, 60, 153
skills-sensory-motor skills 113, 116
social and emotional learning (SEL) 33, 58, 123, 151
social and emotional skills (SES) 56, 123, 152

sociocultural 43, 64
Socrates 7, 26, 27, 91
speaking
    accuracy 44, 53, 61, 62, 110, 113, 149
    freer debate 67, 115, 138
    freer speaking 42, 59, 74
strengths
    cognitive 82, 119
    weaknesses 119
stress
    negative 57, 70, 72, 75, 82, 112, 113, 114, 148
    positive 84
student-centred teaching 17, 18, 20, 21, 36, 42, 94
subjective sense 4
syllabi
    analytic syllabus 18, 39
    synthetic syllabus 18

teacher
    teacher attitude 61
    teaching style 61, 125
teaching
    relaxation & mindfulness 60

teaching methods 15, 16, 23, 42, 45
technology, the role of 8, 23, 150
textbooks 41, 132, 146
Thematic Universe 103, 105, 119, 122
thinking
    critical thinking 12, 26, 30, 49, 52, 104
Thomism 7
tolerance 94
topics – (curriculum)
    and social relevance 45
    topic selection 66, 106
traditional education 11
turn taking 67, 74, 92, 96

University students 64, 65

voice
    evolution of ELT 24
    and I.R.F 44
    learner 53, 132
    state schools 3, 11, 152
Vygotsky 17, 37, 58, 127, 38, 57, 124

Western world 7, 13
whole person model 58, 91, 95

www.ingramcontent.com/pod-product-compliance
Lightning Source LLC
Chambersburg PA
CBHW052126300426
44116CB00010B/1796